Daily
Devotions
for the
ANXIOUS
HEART

Daily
Devotions
for the
ANXIOUS
HEART

*Encouragement and Grace
to Soothe Your Soul*

BARBOUR
PUBLISHING

ecpa
Member of the
Evangelical Christian
Publishers Association

Printed in China.

INTRODUCTION

This lovely daily devotional offers just-right-sized readings to soothe your anxious heart.

The 365 devotional readings feature important-to-you themes—from Blessings to Contentment, Friendship to Hope, Renewal to Truth and Wisdom. . .and dozens more.

As you move through the pages of *Daily Devotions for the Anxious Heart*, you'll be encouraged and inspired every day of the year as you experience the refreshing assurance and comfort that can be found only through an intimate relationship with the Master Creator.

Be blessed!

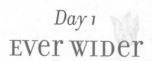

Day 1
ever wider

A longing fulfilled is a tree of life.
PROVERBS 13:12

Take stock of your life. What were you most hoping to achieve a year ago (or five years ago)? How many of those goals have been achieved? Sometimes, once we reach a goal, we move on too quickly to the next one, never allowing ourselves to find the grace God wants to reveal within that achievement. With each goal reached, His grace spreads into your life, like a tree whose branches grow ever wider.

Day 2
IN HIS HANDS

Do not be anxious about anything,
but in every situation, by prayer and petition,
with thanksgiving, present your requests to God.
PHILIPPIANS 4:6

Need a sure cure for anxiety? Start praying. As you trust that God has your best interests at heart, no matter what situation you face, His peace can replace concern. God says there's nothing you need to worry about. Just put all your troubles in His hands, and He who rules universe upon universe yet knows each hair on your head will see that everything works out right. Are you ready to trust now?

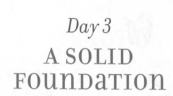

Day 3
A SOLID FOUNDATION

A bad motive can't achieve a good end.
PROVERBS 17:20 MSG

We hear it all the time: the end justifies the means. But that's not how it works in the kingdom of God. It's like trying to build a beautiful house on a shaky foundation—it just doesn't work. Sooner or later, the weak foundation will affect the rest of the house. True achievement is built on God's grace and love. That is the kind of foundation that holds solid no matter what.

Day 4
TODAY!

"Therefore do not worry about tomorrow,
for tomorrow will worry about itself.
Each day has enough trouble of its own."
MATTHEW 6:34

You can look ahead and obsess about fears for
the future or take life one day at a time and
enjoy it. But you only live in today, not in the
weeks, months, and years that may lie ahead.
You can only change life in the moment you're
in right now. Since worry never improves the
future and only hurts today, you'll benefit most
from trusting in God and enjoying the spot
where He's planted you for now.

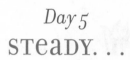

Day 5
STEADY. . .

People with their minds set on you,
you keep completely whole, steady on their feet,
because they keep at it and don't quit.
ISAIAH 26:3 MSG

One of the meanings of *grace* is "an effortless beauty of movement." A person with this kind of grace doesn't trip over her own feet. She's not clumsy or awkward; instead, she moves easily, fluidly, steadily. From a spiritual perspective, most of us stumble quite a bit—and yet we don't give up. We know that God holds our hands, and He will keep us steady even when we would otherwise fall flat on our faces.

Day 6
CHRIST-BALANCE

*Jesus caught them off balance with his
own test question: "What do you think
about the Christ? Whose son is he?"*

MATTHEW 22:41 MSG

Sometimes Christ asks us to find new ways of
thinking. . .new ways of living. . .new ways of
encountering Him in the world around us. That
is not always easy. We don't like to be caught
off-balance. When our life's equilibrium is
shaken, we feel anxious, out of control. But if
we rely on Christ, He will pick us up, dust us
off, and give us the grace to find our balance
in Him.

Day 7
FOCUS POINT

Therefore. . .stand firm.
Let nothing move you.
1 Corinthians 15:58

Some days stress comes at us from all direc-
tions. Our emotions are overwhelming. Life
makes us dizzy. On days like that, don't worry
about getting a lot accomplished—and don't
try to make enormous leaps in your spiritual
life. Instead, simply stand in one place. Like a
ballet dancer who looks at one point to keep her
balance while she twirls, fix your eyes on Jesus.

Day 8
GOD IS IN CONTROL

"Can any one of you by worrying add a single hour to your life?"
MATTHEW 6:27

What does worry gain us? It can't change the length of our days except to decrease the health of our bodies. Ultimately, worry is the most self-defeating thing we can engage in. Besides, why should we give in to concern when God controls our lives? He will always set us on the right path, so we don't have to agonize over life's details.

Day 9
INTEGRITY

*People with integrity walk safely, but those
who follow crooked paths will be exposed.*
PROVERBS 10:9 NLT

Achieving balance in life is seldom easy. We're
likely to go too far—first in one direction and
then another. But despite our tendency to wob-
ble, God's grace always leads us forward. He
keeps us from staggering too far off the path.
As we follow Him, choosing a path of integrity
rather than one of selfishness and lies, we will
find our way easier, our footing surer, and our
balance steadier.

Day 10
SHARING
WITH JESUS

Casting all your care upon him;
for he careth for you.

1 PETER 5:7 KJV

You don't have a care in the world that you
cannot share—with Jesus, that is. There isn't
one thing He doesn't want to hear about from
you. Before you ask a friend to pray for you (and
you should do that), be certain you share your
care with your best Friend, Jesus. Your human
friend may try to help you and may do a lot for
you, but no one helps like Jesus. There's no
worry He can't alleviate or remove.

Day 11
DEEPEST TRUTHS

*For the word of God is alive and powerful.
It is sharper than the sharpest two-edged
sword, cutting between soul and spirit,
between joint and marrow. It exposes
our innermost thoughts and desires.*

HEBREWS 4:12 NLT

God's words are not merely letters on a page.
They are living things that work their way into
our hearts and minds, revealing the fears and
hopes we've kept hidden away, sometimes even
from ourselves. Like a doctor's scalpel that cuts
in order to heal, God's Word slices through
our carefully created facades and exposes our
deepest truths.

Day 12
JUST WHAT
WE NEED

*God can pour on the blessings in
astonishing ways so that you're ready
for anything and everything, more than
just ready to do what needs to be done.*

2 CORINTHIANS 9:8 MSG

Blessings are God's grace visible to us in tangible form. Sometimes they are so small we nearly overlook them—the sun on our faces, the smile of a friend, or food on the table—but other times they amaze us. Day by day, God's grace makes us ready for whatever comes our way. He gives us exactly what we need.

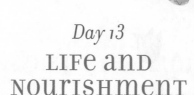

Day 13
LIFE and NOURISHMENT

"I, the Lord, am the one who answers your prayers and watches over you. I am like a green pine tree; your blessings come from me."
HOSEA 14:8 NCV

Think of it: God is like a tree growing at the center of your life! In the shade of this tree, you find shelter. This tree is ever green, with deep roots that draw up life and nourishment. Each one of life's daily blessings is the fruit of this tree. It is the source of all your life, all your joy, and all your being.

Day 14
HOLD ON TO HOPE

The prospect of the righteous is joy,
but the hopes of the wicked come to nothing.

PROVERBS 10:28

Trusting in Jesus gave you new life and hope
for eternity. So how do you respond when
life becomes dark and dull? Does hope slip
away? When no obviously great spiritual
works are going on, do not assume God has
deserted you. Hold on to Him even more
firmly, and trust He will keep His promises.
Truly, what other option do you have? Without Him, hope disappears.

Day 15
WALK CONFIDENTLY

*"But blessed are those who trust
in the Lord and have made the
Lord their hope and confidence."*
JEREMIAH 17:7 NLT

What gives you confidence? Is it your clothes. . .
your money. . .your skills? These are all good
things, but they are blessings from God, given
to you through His grace. When your hopes
(in other words, your expectations for the
future) rest only in God, then you can walk
confidently, knowing He will never disap-
point you.

Day 16
A GIFT

*Don't you see that
children are GOD's best gift?*
PSALM 127:3 MSG

Whether we have children of our own or enjoy others' children, God's grace is revealed to us in a special way through these small people. In children, we catch a glimpse of what God intended for us all—before we grew up and let life cloud our hearts. Children's hope gives us grown-ups hope as well. Their laughter makes us smile, and their love reminds us that we too are loved by God.

Day 17
AN OBEDIENT LIFE

Blessed are those whose way is blameless,
who walk in the Law of the LORD.
PSALM 119:1 NASB

Want to be blessed? Then don't live a sin-filled life. God can't pour out blessings on anyone who consistently ignores His commands. Blessings belong to those who hear God's Word and take it to heart, living it out in love. Want to be blessed? Obey the Master. You'll live blamelessly and joyfully.

Day 18
SMALL THINGS

*"The greatest among you must
become like the youngest."*
LUKE 22:26 NRSV

In some ways, we need to look to children as our role models. We get so used to functioning in the adult world, loaded down with responsibilities, that we forget the child's knack for living in the present moment, for taking delight in small things, for loving unconditionally. Jesus asks us to let go of our grown-up dignity and allow ourselves to enter into His presence as children. When we do, we encounter His grace anew.

Day 19
LOOK UP!

The heavens declare the glory of God;
the skies proclaim the work of his hands.

PSALM 19:1

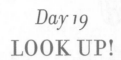

Grace is as near as the sky over your head. Look up and be reminded of how wonderful God truly is. The same God who created the sun and the atmosphere, the stars and the galaxies, the same God who day by day creates a new sunrise and a new sunset, that same God loves you and creates beauty in your life each day!

Day 20
BEAUTIFUL WORLD

*"Walk out into the fields
and look at the wildflowers."*
MATTHEW 6:28 MSG

Take the time to go outdoors. Look at nature.
You don't have to spend hours to realize how
beautiful God made the world. A single flower,
if you really look at it, could be enough to fill
you with awe. Sometimes we only need something very simple to remind us of God's grace.

Day 21
GOD OF COMFORT

[God] comforts us in all our troubles,
so that we can comfort those in any trouble
with the comfort we. . .receive from God.

2 CORINTHIANS 1:4

When you hurt, God offers you comfort. No
trouble is so large or so small that He will not
help. But when you have received His strength
for the trouble at hand, do you share it in
turn? Comfort isn't meant to be hidden away;
it should be passed on to those in a similar
need. As part of the body of Christ, we—the
church—should be sharing the knowledge
that God cares for and strengthens all His
children.

Day 22
LAW OF LOVE

*I pondered the direction of my life,
and I turned to follow your laws.*
PSALM 119:59 NLT

Did you know that the word *law* comes from
root words that mean "foundation" or "something firm and fixed"? Sometimes we can't
help but feel confused and uncertain. When
that happens, turn to God's law, His rule for
living. Love is His law, the foundation that
always holds firm. When we cling to that, we
find direction.

Day 23
GRACE FOR EACH DAY

May the Lord direct your hearts into
God's love and Christ's perseverance.
2 THESSALONIANS 3:5

Allow God to lead you each day. His grace will lead you deeper and deeper into the love of God—a love that heals your wounds and works through you to touch those around you. Just as Christ never gave up but let love lead Him all the way to the cross, so too will God direct you all the way, giving you the strength and the courage you need to face each challenge.

Day 24
CLOSER TO HIM

"When the Spirit of truth comes, he will guide
you into all truth. He will not speak on his
own but will tell you what he has heard."
JOHN 16:13 NLT

God's Spirit is truth. In Him there are no lies.
You can trust Him absolutely to lead you ever
closer to God. This is how you recognize true
grace: it will always bring you nearer to the One
who loves you most, the God who created you
and gave Himself for you. If you find yourself
somewhere else, you have not been following
the Spirit.

Day 25
REACHING OUT

*For just as we share abundantly in
the sufferings of Christ, so also our
comfort abounds through Christ.*

2 CORINTHIANS 1:5

Paul knew the pain of persecution, but he also
knew the deep comfort God offered. When
people gave the apostle trouble, God drew
His servant close to His heart. When trials
come your way, God will do the same for you.
If life is always going smoothly, comfort is
meaningless; but when you're in the midst
of trouble, He comes alongside with tender
love that overflows your trials and reaches
out to others.

Day 26
LEADING

But since we belong to the day, let us be sober,
putting on faith and love as a breastplate,
and the hope of salvation as a helmet.

1 THESSALONIANS 5:8

We sometimes think of discipline as a negative thing, as something that asks us to sacrifice and punish ourselves. But really the word has more to do with the grace we receive from instruction and learning, from following a master. Like an athlete who follows her coach's leading, we are called to follow our Master, wearing His uniform of love and His helmet of hope.

Day 27
FOLLOW JESUS

*"Whoever serves me must follow me;
and where I am, my servant also will be.
My Father will honor the one who serves me."*

JOHN 12:26

A disciple is someone who follows. That is
the discipline we practice: we follow Jesus.
Wherever He is, we go. In His presence, we
find the daily grace we need to live. As we serve
Him, God honors us; He affirms our dignity
and makes us all we were meant to be.

Day 28
RENEWAL OF FAITH

*"As one whom his mother comforts,
so I will comfort you."*
ISAIAH 66:13 NKJV

Like a tender mother, God comforts His people. When life challenges us, we have a place to renew our faith. Instead of questioning God's compassion because we face a trial, we can draw ever nearer to Him, seeking to do His will. Surrounded by His tender arms, we gain strength to go out and face the world again.

Day 29
GOD'S PROVISION

*Now godliness with
contentment is great gain.*
1 TIMOTHY 6:6 NKJV

Paul warned Timothy against false teachers
who wanted to use the church for financial
gain. If these people were looking for security, they were on the wrong track. Money,
which comes and goes, never brings real protection. Our security lies in God's provision.
Whether or not we have a large bank account,
we can feel content in Jesus. The One who
brought us into this world will never forget we
require food, clothing, and all the rest. When
we truly trust in Jesus, contentment is sure
to follow.

Day 30
CHRISTLIKE

Don't sin by letting anger control you.
Think about it overnight and remain silent.
PSALM 4:4 NLT

A disciple must practice certain skills until she becomes good at them. As Christ's disciples, we are called to live like Him. The challenge of that calling is often hardest in life's small, daily frustrations, especially with the people we love the most. But as we practice saying no to anger, controlling it rather than allowing it to control us, God's grace helps us develop new skills, even ones we never thought possible!

Day 31
LIFe's circumstances

My child, do not reject the LORD's discipline,
and don't get angry when he corrects you.
The LORD corrects those he loves, just as
parents correct the child they delight in.

PROVERBS 3:11–12 NCV

God doesn't send us to time-out, and He
certainly doesn't take us over His knee and
spank us. Instead, His discipline comes to us
through the circumstances of life. By saying
yes to whatever we face, no matter how difficult and frustrating it may be, we allow God's
grace to infuse each moment of our day. We
may be surprised to find that even in life's
most discouraging moments, God's love was
waiting all along.

Day 32
REACH OUT TO HIM

*"Your words have supported those
who were falling; you encouraged
those with shaky knees."*

JOB 4:4 NLT

God knows how weak and shaky we feel some
days. He understands our feelings. After all,
He made us, so He understands how prone
humans are to discouragement. He doesn't
blame us for being human, but He never leaves
us helpless, either. His grace is always there,
like a hand held out to us, simply waiting for
us to reach out and grasp it.

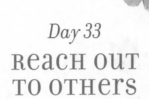

Day 33
REACH OUT TO OTHERS

Whoever has the gift of encouraging others should encourage.

ROMANS 12:8 NCV

Just as God encourages us, He wants us to encourage others. The word *encourage* comes from Latin words that mean "to put heart or inner strength into someone." When God encourages us, His own heart reaches out to us, and His strength becomes ours. As we rely on His grace, we are empowered to turn and reach out to those around us, lending them our hearts and strength.

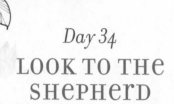

Day 34
LOOK TO THE SHEPHERD

The LORD is my shepherd,
I lack nothing.
PSALM 23:1

No matter your physical circumstances, if Jesus is your Shepherd, you never have to want spiritually. No matter what the world throws at you, you can be at peace. No fear overcomes those who follow the Shepherd as their King. He guides them through every trial, leading them faithfully into an eternity with Him. Are you lacking contentment today? Look to the Shepherd for peace.

Day 35
WATCHFUL LOVE

I have learned in whatever
state I am, to be content.
PHILIPPIANS 4:11 NKJV

Paul wasn't writing about a grit-your-teeth kind of contentment. He had learned to trust deeply in God for all his needs, so the apostle did not worry about future events. His strength lay in God, who cared for his every need, even when churches forgot him.

We too can be content in Jesus. If the boss doesn't give us a raise or an unexpected bill comes in, He knows it. Nothing escapes His watchful love in our lives.

Day 36
Reciprocal

When we get together, I want to
encourage you in your faith, but I
also want to be encouraged by yours.
ROMANS 1:12 NLT

Encouragement is always reciprocal. When
we encourage others, we are ourselves encouraged. In the world's economy, we pay a
price in order to receive something we want;
in other words, we give up something to get
something. But in God's economy, we always
get back what we give up. We are connected
to each other, like parts of a body. Whatever
good things we do for another are good for us
as well.

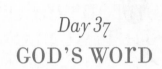

Day 37
GOD'S WORD

I weep with sorrow;
encourage me by your word.
PSALM 119:28 NLT

Tears come easily some days. The world is full of pain and darkness, and we feel helpless. Those are the days when we need to turn to God's Word for encouragement. We may not be able to sense His grace in our lives, but we will always find it in the Bible's pages.

Day 38
CONTENTMENT
IN TROUBLE

The fear of the LORD leads to life; then one rests content, untouched by trouble.
PROVERBS 19:23

God doesn't promise we will never suffer trouble, but He does promise something even more important. In the middle of trouble, we will experience real life—contentment in the middle of confusion, doubt, or turmoil. Which would you prefer, trouble and life in Jesus or trouble on its own? You can't avoid trouble here on earth. But share life with Him, and contentment will follow.

Day 39
BY HIS GRACE

A person is made right with God through faith,
not through obeying the law.
ROMANS 3:28 NCV

Human laws can never make us into the people
we are meant to be. No matter how scrupulous
we try to be, we will always fall short. Our hands
and hearts will come up empty. But as we fix
our eyes on God, committing our lives and
ourselves to Him, we are made right. We are
healed and made whole by His grace, exactly
as God meant us to be.

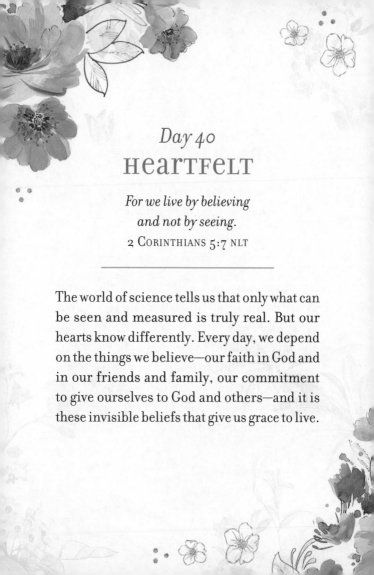

Day 40
HEARTFELT

*For we live by believing
and not by seeing.*
2 CORINTHIANS 5:7 NLT

The world of science tells us that only what can
be seen and measured is truly real. But our
hearts know differently. Every day, we depend
on the things we believe—our faith in God and
in our friends and family, our commitment
to give ourselves to God and others—and it is
these invisible beliefs that give us grace to live.

Day 41
UNFAILING LOVE

But I trust in your unfailing love.
I will rejoice because you have rescued me.
PSALM 13:5 NLT

Have you ever done that exercise in trust where you fall backward into another person's arms? It's hard to let yourself drop, trusting that the other person will catch you. The decision to let yourself fall is not an emotion that sweeps over you. It's just something you have to do, despite your fear. In the same way, we commit ourselves to God's unfailing love, finding new joy each time His arms keep us from falling.

Day 42
SAFE IN CHRIST

This is what God commands: that we
believe in his Son, Jesus Christ, and that
we love each other, just as he commanded.
1 JOHN 3:23 NCV

Again and again, the Bible links faith and love. Our human tendency is to put up walls of selfishness around ourselves to protect ourselves at all costs. God asks us instead to believe daily that we are safe in Christ and to allow ourselves to be vulnerable as we reach out in love to those around us.

Day 43
ETERNAL PERSPECTIVE

"Where, O death, is your victory?
Where, O death, is your sting?"
1 CORINTHIANS 15:55

Nothing in this world ameliorates the pain of death. Losing one we love reaches deep into our souls. But with His sacrifice, Jesus permanently overcame the sting of mortality. Those who trust in Him do not live for a few short years, but for eternity. When sin takes their lives, they simply move into heaven. When we lose loved ones, our hearts feel pain. But if they gave their lives to Jesus, He is still victorious. In time, we will meet them again.

Day 44
OUR HOPE

God raised him from the dead, freeing him
from the agony of death, because it was
impossible for death to keep its hold on him.
ACTS 2:24

Death could not grasp Jesus, the sinless One
who died for the guilty. Though it clings to
sinful beings, it had no claim on God's Son.
Jesus is our only hope. Though sin deserves
death, God's compassion made a way to free
us from its agonies. When we give our poor,
mortal lives to Jesus, we rise in Him, sharing
His eternal life.

Day 45
STICKING TOGETHER

*Families stick together
in all kinds of trouble.*
PROVERBS 17:17 MSG

Families can drive you crazy. Whether it's the
people with whom you share a house or the
extended family that gets together at holidays
and birthdays, family members can be exas-
perating, even infuriating. When it comes
right down to it, though, your family members
are the ones who show you God's grace even
when life is hard, the ones who stick by you
no matter what (even when they make you
crazy!).

Day 46
"EXTENDED" FAMILY

God sets the lonely in families.
PSALM 68:6

God knows that we need others. We need their love and support, their understanding, and their simple physical presence nearby. That is why He gives us families. Families don't need to be related by blood, though. They might be the people you work with, or the people you go to church with, or the group of friends you've known since grade school. Whoever they are, they're the people who make God's grace real to you every day.

Day 47
THE ONLY WAY

"I am the way and the truth and the life.
No one comes to the Father except through me."
JOHN 14:6

Plenty of people doubt Jesus. But those who have accepted Him as their Savior need not wallow in uncertainty. His Spirit speaks to ours, moment by moment, if we will only listen. He tells us God has shown us the way; we need not seek another path or truth. No other road leads to God. For a vibrant Christian life, we simply need to continue down the highway we're traveling with Jesus.

Day 48
BE FAITHFUL

Good and upright is the LORD;
therefore he instructs sinners in his ways.

PSALM 25:8

Don't know which way to turn or where to go?
God will show you. Just be faithful to Him,
and you will hear His still, small voice guiding you. Otherwise, circumstances and wise
advisors will illuminate the path you need to
take. Still doubting? Ask God for forgiveness
for sins that bar your communion with Him.
Soon, with a clean heart, you'll be headed in
the right direction.

Day 49
MOVING MOUNTAINS

"Whoever says to this mountain, 'Be removed and be cast into the sea,' and does not doubt. . . but believes. . .will have whatever he says."
MARK 11:23 NKJV

Don't you wish you had faith like this? Christians often try to gear up to it, willing it with all their hearts. But that's not what God had in mind. Manipulating Him cannot work.

Only when we fully trust in Him will He move our mountain—even if it's in an unexpected direction.

Day 50
FAMILY TIES

Jesus, who makes people holy, and those who are made holy are from the same family. So he is not ashamed to call them his brothers and sisters.

HEBREWS 2:11 NCV

You and Jesus are family! Jesus, the One who made you whole and clean in God's sight, is your Brother. Family ties connect you to Him and to all those with whom He is connected. In Christ, we find new connections with each other. By His grace, we are now kinfolk.

Day 51
GROUNDED IN LOVE

"You'll be built solid, grounded in righteousness, far from any trouble—nothing to fear!"

ISAIAH 54:12 MSG

Balance isn't something we can achieve in ourselves. Just when we think we have it all together, life tends to come crashing down around our ears. But even in the middle of life's most chaotic moments, God gives us grace. He keeps us balanced in His love. Like a building that is built to sway in an earthquake without falling down, we will stay standing if we remain grounded in His love.

Day 52
GOD'S PLAN

My dear brothers and sisters, take note of
this: Everyone should be quick to listen,
slow to speak and slow to become angry.

JAMES 1:19

God gives good advice on anger. Often, if we listen carefully and hold our tongues, we don't become angry in the first place. Good communication forestalls a lot of emotional trauma. Hurt emotions often cause us to speak words we regret, simply making the problem worse. So when we feel tempted to anger, let's stop, listen, and hold our tongues for a while. That's God's plan for more peaceful relationships.

Day 53
GENTLE SPEECH

A gentle answer turns away wrath,
but a harsh word stirs up anger.

PROVERBS 15:1

How you speak can strongly affect those around you. If someone is hot under the collar, do you quell that anger with calming words or inflame him with harsh ones? Do you start a forest fire with your sister who irritates you or quench the blaze with soft words? Anger's heat makes wise decision making impossible. But God's Word offers advice that brings peace to our lives. Gentle speech leads to wiser choices.

Day 54
BLESSING OTHERS

We work hard with our own hands.
When we are cursed, we bless;
when we are persecuted, we endure it.

1 CORINTHIANS 4:12

God gave Paul many blessings, and the apostle passed them on, even if the recipients didn't seem to really deserve them. Those who cursed him (and they were, no doubt, many) did not receive a cursing in return. Instead, Paul tried to bless them. Do we follow the apostle's example? When we are cursed by the words of others, what is our response?

Day 55
LIVING FOR CHRIST

*If you live according to the flesh, you will
die; but if by the Spirit you put to death
the misdeeds of the body, you will live.*
ROMANS 8:13

Living for Christ through His Spirit offers
real life, overflowing and abundant. Blessings
spill over in obedient lives. But the world, at
war with God, doesn't understand. Unbelievers never feel the touch of the Spirit in their
hearts and lives, and Jesus' gentle love is for-
eign to them. Put to death worldly misdeeds,
and instead of the emptiness of the world,
you'll receive blessings indeed.

Day 56
A GODLY EXAMPLE

*"Let the little children come to Me,
and do not forbid them; for of
such is the kingdom of heaven."*
MATTHEW 19:14 NKJV

On earth, Jesus loved children. He never shut them out. Though their youth gave them little credence in Israel, He saw the faith potential in them. Certainly the children loved Jesus too, for His kindheartedness. Do we shut children out of our lives because we are too busy or have more "important" things on our minds? Then we need to take an example from Jesus. For a new take on God's kingdom, spend time with a child today.

Day 57
GIVER OF COMFORT

You ought to forgive and comfort him,
so that he will not be overwhelmed
by excessive sorrow.
2 CORINTHIANS 2:7

Do you know someone who is sorry for her sin? Then don't keep reminding her of it. If she has sought forgiveness and put it behind her, it is dead. Instead of criticizing, remind her of the power of God that works in her life. Encourage her when temptation calls her name. Then she will not be overcome by sorrow and fall into sin again. Give comfort, and you will be a blessing.

Day 58
GOD'S PROMISE

*This is the promise that He
has promised us—eternal life.*
1 JOHN 2:25 NKJV

The promise of eternal life comes straight
from God. Those who receive Jesus into their
hearts do not end their existence when they
stop breathing. Their last breath on earth is
merely a precursor of life in eternity with Jesus.
Today you miss the one you lost, and your heart
aches. But in eternity, you will be reunited and
will share the joys of death conquered by the
Savior. Until you meet again, simply trust in
His unfailing promise.

Day 59
SHARING
OUR FAITH

*[And I pray] that the participation in
and sharing of your faith may produce and
promote full recognition and appreciation and
understanding and precise knowledge of every
good [thing] that is ours in [our identification
with] Christ Jesus [and unto His glory].*

PHILEMON 1:6 AMPC

Many of us have a hard time sharing our faith.
So when we hear Paul's encouragement to
Philemon, our hearts lift, knowing we aren't
the only ones who struggle. Isn't the challenge of witnessing to others worth it, once
we understand this promise? The salvation
of others and our own thorough appreciation
of our Lord: could we have better reasons to
share His love?

Day 60
NO DIVISION

*In Christ's family there can be no division
into Jew and non-Jew, slave and free,
male and female. Among us you are all equal.*
GALATIANS 3:28 MSG

Grace is a gift that none of us deserves—and by grace Jesus has removed all barriers between God and ourselves. God asks that, as members of His family, we also knock down all the walls we've built between ourselves and others. Not just the obvious ones, but also the ones that may hide in our blind spots. In Christ, there is no liberal or conservative, no educated or uneducated, no division whatsoever.

Day 61
COMPASSION

Be merciful to those who doubt.
JUDE 22

If you've ever doubted (as we all have), you can understand why this verse is in the Bible. If well-meaning folks attacked you for your uncertainty, it probably didn't help—they just made you more nervous. When questions enter our minds, we need someone encouraging to come alongside us and provide answers, not a critic who wants to condemn our feelings. Knowing that, we also need compassion for other doubters. May we be the merciful ones who aid those doubting hearts.

Day 62
SENSITIVITY

*At the same time, don't be callous in
your exercise of freedom, thoughtlessly
stepping on the toes of those who aren't
as free as you are. I try my best to be
considerate of everyone's feelings in all
these matters; I hope you will be, too.*

1 CORINTHIANS 10:32–33 MSG

The person who walks in grace doesn't trip over
other people's feet. She doesn't shove her way
through life like a bull in a china shop. Instead,
she allows the grace she has so freely received
to make her more aware of others' feelings.
With God-given empathy, she is sensitive to
those around her, sharing the grace she has
received with all she meets.

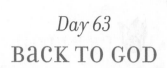

Day 63
BACK TO GOD

My dear brothers and sisters, always be willing to listen and slow to speak. Do not become angry easily, because anger will not help you live the right kind of life God wants.
JAMES 1:19–20 NCV

Our feelings are gifts from God, and we should never be ashamed of them. Instead, we need to offer them all back to God, both our joys and our frustrations. When we give God our anger, our irritation, our hurt feelings, and our frustrations, we make room in our hearts to truly hear what others are saying.

Day 64
PERCEPTION

"The LORD himself goes before you and will be with you; he will never leave you nor forsake you. Do not be afraid; do not be discouraged."

DEUTERONOMY 31:8

The world we see with our eyes is only a piece of reality, a glimpse into an enormous and mysterious universe. Just as our eyes often deceive us, so do our feelings. We perceive life through our emotions, but they are as limited as our physical vision. Whether we sense God's presence or not, He is always with us. Grace waits to meet us in the future, so we can disregard all our feelings of fear and discouragement.

Day 65
LETTING GO

A peaceful heart leads to a healthy body;
jealousy is like cancer in the bones.
PROVERBS 14:30 NLT

Some emotions are meant to be nourished,
and others need to be quickly dropped into
God's hands. Learn to cultivate and seek out
that which brings peace to your heart. And
practice letting go of your negative feelings
as quickly as you can, releasing them to God.
If you cling to these dark feelings, they will
reproduce like a cancer, blocking the healthy
flow of grace into your life.

Day 66
BE PREPARED

He has also set eternity in the human heart;
yet no one can fathom what God has
done from beginning to end.

ECCLESIASTES 3:11

Though each of us has a bit of eternity in our hearts, and we cannot rest unless we know the Savior, we also cannot fathom the works of God. That can either make us dissatisfied and doubtful or relaxed, trusting children who know their Father is in control and will care for them from beginning to end. Have you trusted Him who is the Alpha and Omega? Are you prepared for eternity with Him?

Day 67
ALWAYS SECURE

Your throne was established long ago;
you are from all eternity.
PSALM 93:2

There was never a moment when God did not exist. No scrap of time or eternity came into being without Him, and nothing escapes His powerful reign. That's good news for His children. For whatever we face now or in our heavenly abode, we know our Father is in control. No spiritual warfare or earthly disaster lies beyond His plan. No wickedness of Satan can take Him by surprise. Ours is the eternal Lord, who has loved us from the start. In Him, we are always secure.

Day 68

UNCHANGING

Your word, LORD, is eternal;
it stands firm in the heavens.
PSALM 119:89

The Word of God never changes. The Father's commands do not alter, and neither does Jesus, the Word made flesh, or His promise of salvation. Those who trust in Him are secure as the Lord Himself, for He does not change, and none of His promises pass away unfulfilled. The eternal Lord and all He commands stand firm. To gain eternity, simply receive Christ as your Savior; then trust in Him.

Day 69
PURE DELIGHT

You make known to me the path of life;
you will fill me with joy in your presence,
with eternal pleasures at your right hand.

PSALM 16:11

Rejoicing in God? Those who do not know Jesus cannot imagine it. You have to know Jesus to delight in His presence, just as you cannot enjoy a friend until you come to know each other and enjoy companionship. But knowing and loving God brings us, His children, joy in His presence and the prospect of undefined pleasures at His side. Are you prepared to share those joys with Jesus for eternity?

Day 70
TRUE
NOURISHMENT

He gives food to every living thing.
His faithful love endures forever.
PSALM 136:25 NLT

People often have a confused relationship with
food. We love to eat, but we feel guilty when
we do. We sometimes turn to food when we're
tense or worried, trying to fill the empty, anxious holes in our hearts. But God wants to give
us the true nourishment we need, body and
soul, if only we will let Him.

Day 71
DAILY MIRACLES

*"That is why I tell you not to worry
about everyday life—whether you have
enough food and drink, or enough
clothes to wear. Isn't life more than food,
and your body more than clothing?"*
MATTHEW 6:25 NLT

With our eyes fixed on what we *don't* have,
we often overlook the grace we have already
received. God has blessed us in many ways.
Our bodies function day after day in amazing
ways we take for granted, and life is filled with
an abundance of daily miracles. Why do we
worry so much about the details when we live
in such a vast sea of daily grace?

Day 72
GOD'S HONOR

For the honor of your name,
O Lord, forgive my many, many sins.
PSALM 25:11 NLT

Like all gifts of grace, forgiveness by its very definition is nothing that can ever be earned. Forgiveness is what God gives us when we deserve nothing but anger. He forgives us not because we merit it, but because of His own honor. Over and over, we will turn away from God; but over and over, He will bring us back. That is who He is!

Day 73
WHOLLY and COMPLETELY

"Forgive others, and you will be forgiven."
LUKE 6:37 NLT

The words *forgive* and *pardon* come from very
old words that mean "to give up completely
and wholeheartedly." When we forgive others,
we totally give up our rights to feel we've been
injured or slighted. In return, God's grace
totally fills the gaps left behind when we let go
of our own selfishness. As we give ourselves
wholeheartedly to others, God gives Himself
completely to us.

Day 74
LaVISH and
ABUNDANT

Let them come back to GOD, who is
merciful, come back to our God,
who is lavish with forgiveness.

ISAIAH 55:7 MSG

God's forgiveness is never stingy or grudg-
ing. He never waits to offer it to us. Instead,
it's always there, a lavish, abundant flood of
grace just waiting for us to turn away from our
sin and accept it.

Day 75
SOURCE OF
SALVATION

*He became the source of eternal
salvation for all who obey him.*

HEBREWS 5:9

Salvation in Jesus is important to our earthly
lives. How many times has He dispelled danger or helped us avoid it? How often has sin
failed to mar our lives because we obeyed His
commands? But Jesus is also the source of
salvation in eternity. Instead of remaining
forever in our earthly lives, God planned to
bring us into everlasting life with Him, in His
restored kingdom. In heaven, we will praise
His salvation without end.

Day 76
LOVING JESUS

*Looking unto Jesus the author
and finisher of our faith.*
HEBREWS 12:2 KJV

God is writing a story of faith through your life.
What will it describe? Will it be a chronicle of
challenges overcome, like the Old Testament
story of Joseph? Or a near tragedy turned into
joy, like that of the prodigal son? Whatever
your account says, if you love Jesus, the end is
never in question. Those who love Him finish in heaven despite their trials on earth.
The long, weary path ends in His arms. Today,
write a chapter in your faithful narrative of
God's love.

Day 77
HE NEVER FAILS

If we are faithless, he remains faithful,
for he cannot disown himself.

2 TIMOTHY 2:13

Sometimes our faith fails, but Jesus never does. When we change for the worse, slip, or make a mistake, He is still the same faithful God He's always been. Though we may falter, He cannot. If we give in to the tempter's wiles, let us turn again to the faithful One. If we have trusted in Him, we can turn to Him for renewed forgiveness. His own faithfulness will not allow Him to deny us.

Day 78
perfection

*His works are perfect, and all his
ways are just. A faithful God who
does no wrong, upright and just is he.*

DEUTERONOMY 32:4

Many unbelievers, or even weakening believers living in crisis, complain that God is unfair. But Moses, who suffered much for God's people, knew better than that. God is always perfect, faithful, and just—it's rebellious humanity that lacks these qualities.

We can have faith in God's perfection. He's never failed His people yet, though they have often been false. Trust in Him today. As He led His people to the promised land, He'll lead you home to Himself.

Day 79
SPIRITUAL CERTAINTY

We live by faith, not by sight.
2 CORINTHIANS 5:7

There is more than one way of seeing. We view the world around us with our eyes, but by doing so, we don't apprehend all there is in life. Those things we "see" by faith cannot be envisioned by our physical eyes. That's why doubters disbelieve them. But when God speaks to our hearts, it is as real as if we'd viewed the truth plainly in front of us. Like Paul, though our eyes cannot see it, we have a spiritual certainty.

Day 80
unconditional grace

A friend loves at all times.
PROVERBS 17:17 NASB

Friends are the people you can allow to see you at your worst. They're the ones who can see you without your makeup. . .or walk in when your house is a mess. . .or overhear you acting like a thirteen-year-old—and they'll still be your friends. They reveal to you God's unconditional grace.

Day 81
our companion

Our LORD, you are the friend of your worshipers,
and you make an agreement with all of us.
PSALM 25:14 CEV

God is our Friend. He is our Companion
through life's journey. He is the One who
always understands us; and no matter what
we do, He always accepts us and loves us. What
better agreement could we ever have with
anyone than what we have with God?

Day 82
NEVER FAILING...

"My friends scorn me,
but I pour out my tears to God."
JOB 16:20 NLT

Sometimes even your best friends can let
you down. Human beings aren't perfect. But
God's grace will never fail you. When even
your closest friends don't understand you,
take your hurt to Him.

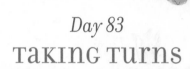

Day 83
TAKING TURNS

Two people are better off than one, for they can help each other succeed. If one person falls, the other can reach out and help. But someone who falls alone is in real trouble.

ECCLESIASTES 4:9–10 NLT

Have you ever noticed that in the best friendships, you take turns being needy? You're strong enough to help your friend one day, and the next day, she's the one offering you comfort and help. Over and over, God uses our friends to make His grace real in our lives. And He wants to use us to spread His grace to our friends.

Day 84
WHAT YOU CRAVE

*Take delight in the LORD, and he
will give you your heart's desires.*
PSALM 37:4 NLT

Do you ever feel as though God wants to deny
you what you want, as though He's a cruel step-
parent who takes pleasure in thwarting you?
That image of God is a lie. He's the One who
placed your heart's desires deep inside you.
As you turn to Him, knowing that He alone
is the source of all true delight, He will grant
you what your heart most truly craves.

Day 85
SATISFIED

Satisfy us in the morning with your
unfailing love, that we may sing for
joy and be glad all our days.

PSALM 90:14

God wants to fulfill you. He wants you to feel
satisfied with life so that you will catch yourself
humming or singing His praises all day long.
Even when life is hard, He is waiting to comfort
you with His unfailing love so that gladness
will creep over your heart once more.

Day 86
THE NEXT OASIS

The LORD will always guide you and
provide good things to eat when you are
in the desert. He will make you healthy.
You will be like a garden that has plenty of
water or like a stream that never runs dry.

ISAIAH 58:11 CEV

God wants you to be healthy—not just physically, but emotionally, intellectually, and spiritually. He wants to fill your life full of all the things you truly need. The life He wants for you is not dry and empty and barren. Instead, it is lush and full of delicious things to nourish you. We all have to cross life's deserts sometimes, but even then, God will supply what you need to reach the next oasis He has waiting.

Day 87
WONDERFUL PLANS

*"For I know the plans I have for you," says
the LORD. "They are plans for good and not
for disaster, to give you a future and a hope."*
JEREMIAH 29:11 NLT

Don't worry about the future. No matter how
frightening it may look to you sometimes,
God is waiting there for you. He has plans for
you, wonderful plans that will lead you deeper
and deeper into His grace and love.

Day 88
safe

My life is in your hands. Save me from
my enemies and from those
who are chasing me.
Psalm 31:15 ncv

Do you ever feel like trouble is chasing you? No matter how fast you run or how you try to hide, it comes relentlessly after you, dogging your footsteps, breathing its hot breath down your neck, robbing you of peace. What's even worse is that it waits for you down the road as well! Maybe you need to stop running and hiding and instead let yourself drop into God's hands, knowing He will hold your future safe.

Day 89
WONDERFUL THINGS

*Everything God made is waiting
with excitement for God to show
his children's glory completely.*
ROMANS 8:19 NCV

Some days it's hard to feel very optimistic.
We listen to the evening news and hear story
after story about natural disasters and human
greed. God doesn't want us to be ostriches,
hiding our heads in the sand, refusing to acknowledge what's going on in the world. But
He also wants us to believe that the future is
full of wonderful things He has planned. The
whole world is holding its breath, waiting for
God's wonderful grace to reveal itself.

Day 90
THE DETAILS

She is clothed with strength and dignity,
and she laughs without fear of the future.
PROVERBS 31:25 NLT

God wants to clothe us with His strength, His dignity. He wants us to be whole and competent, full of His grace. When we are, we can look at the future and laugh, knowing that God will take care of the details as we trust Him to be the foundation of our lives.

Day 91
PRAISE HIM

Let them praise the name of the LORD,
for His name alone is exalted; His glory
is above the earth and heaven.
PSALM 148:13 NKJV

Trusting Jesus gives you a spectacular view of
God's power. His work in your life increasingly opens your eyes to this glorious King
who loves you. But those who do not know
Him cannot praise Him. They are thoroughly
blind to the glories of the One whom they have
denied. Yet in the end, His glory will be ap-
parent even to them. Whom do you follow—
the glorious One or mere humans?

Day 92
our Hearts

Are you willing to acknowledge, you foolish person, that faith without works is useless?
James 2:20 NASB

Faith isn't faith if actions don't follow belief.
No matter what a person says, unless love,
compassion, and kindness accompany her
words, it would be foolish to consider her
Christian testimony believable. Though works
don't save us, they show what's in our hearts.
What are we proving by our works today?

Day 93
HAPPINESS REQUIREMENT...

I'm just as happy with little as with much, with much as with little. I've found the recipe for being happy whether full or hungry, hands full or hands empty. Whatever I have, wherever I am, I can make it through anything in the One who makes me who I am.

<small>PHILIPPIANS 4:12 MSG</small>

When you were younger, what did you think you needed to be happy? Nice clothes? A boyfriend? A husband? A good job? Today, what is it you think your happiness requires? God blesses us daily, but our happiness does not depend on those blessings. Our joy depends only on God. When we realize that, we no longer have to worry about losing or gaining life's blessings.

Day 94
SIMPLY HAPPY

Are any of you happy?
You should sing praises.
JAMES 5:13 NLT

Some days are simply happy days. The sun shines, people make us laugh, and life seems good. A day like that is a special grace. Thank God for it. As you hum through your day, don't forget to sing His praises.

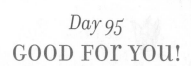

Day 95
GOOD FOR YOU!

A happy heart is like good medicine,
but a broken spirit drains your strength.
PROVERBS 17:22 NCV

God longs to make you happy. He knows
that happiness is good for you. Mentally and
physically, you function better when you are
happy. Discouragement and sadness sap your
strength. It's like trying to work while carrying
a heavy load on your back. It slows you down
and makes everything harder. Let God heal
the breaks in your spirit. His grace can make
you strong and happy.

Day 96
RESCUED!

The Lord wants to show his mercy to you.
He wants to rise and comfort you. The Lord
is a fair God, and everyone who waits
for his help will be happy.
ISAIAH 30:18 NCV

God doesn't want you to feel lonely and unhappy. He waits to bring you close to Him, to
comfort you, to forgive you. Wait for Him to
rescue you from life's unhappiness. His grace
will never let you down. Keep your eyes fixed
on Him, and you will find happiness again.

Day 97
FOR ETERNITY

*My health may fail, and my spirit
may grow weak, but God remains the
strength of my heart; he is mine forever.*
PSALM 73:26 NLT

Sooner or later, our bodies let us down. Even
the healthiest of us will one day have to face
old age. When our bodies' strength fails us,
we may feel discouraged and depressed. But
even then we can find joy and strength in our
God. When our hearts belong to the Creator of
the universe, we realize we are far more than
our bodies. Because of God's unfailing grace,
we will be truly healthy for all eternity.

Day 98
THE ENTIRE PACKAGE

*He makes the whole body fit together
perfectly. As each part does its own
special work, it helps the other parts
grow, so that the whole body is healthy
and growing and full of love.*

EPHESIANS 4:16 NLT

God has a holistic perspective on health. He
sees your body, soul, heart, and mind; and
He wants each part of you to be strong and fit.
He looks at our world in the same way, longing to heal the entire package—society, the
environment, and governments. He wants
His body on earth, the church, to be whole
and strong as well. Health pours out of Him,
a daily stream of grace on which we can rely
for each aspect of life.

Day 99
CHOOSING
CHEERFUL

A cheerful disposition is good for your health;
gloom and doom leave you bone-tired.
PROVERBS 17:22 MSG

Have you ever heard the saying "You may not be able to keep birds from perching on your head, but you can keep them from building nests in your hair"? It means we can't always control our emotions, but we *can* choose which ones we want to hold on to and dwell on. Choosing to be cheerful instead of gloomy is far healthier for our minds, bodies, and spirits. Being depressed is exhausting!

Day 100
WHOLE AND HEALTHY

When Jesus heard this, he told them,
"Healthy people don't need a doctor—
sick people do. I have come to call not
those who think they are righteous,
but those who know they are sinners."

MARK 2:17 NLT

With Jesus, we never need to pretend to be something we aren't. We don't need to impress Him with our spiritual maturity and mental acuity. Instead, we can come to Him honestly, with all our neediness, admitting just how weak we are. When we do, we let down the barriers that keep Him out of our hearts. We allow His grace to make us whole and healthy.

Day 101
Free!

*For the Lord is the Spirit, and wherever
the Spirit of the Lord is, there is freedom.*
2 Corinthians 3:17 nlt

How do you know when the Holy Spirit is present in your life? You should be able to tell by the sense of freedom you feel. If you feel oppressed, obsessed, or depressed, something in your life is out of kilter. Seek out God's Spirit. He wants you to be free.

Day 102
BREATHING

In certain ways we are weak, but the Spirit is here to help us. For example, when we don't know what to pray for, the Spirit prays for us in ways that cannot be put into words.

ROMANS 8:26 CEV

The Holy Spirit is the wind that blows through our world, breathing grace and life into everything that exists. He will breathe through you as well as you open yourself to Him. We need not worry about our own weakness or mistakes, for the Spirit will make up for them. His creative power will pray through us, work through us, and love through us.

Day 103
HIS INSTRUMENT

*"The Spirit of the Lord is on me, because
he has anointed me to proclaim good news
to the poor. He has sent me to proclaim
freedom for the prisoners and recovery of
sight for the blind, to set the oppressed free."*
LUKE 4:18

Just as the Holy Spirit wants you to be free,
He also wants to use you as His instrument to
breathe freedom and hope into the world. Be
His instrument today. Tell people the truly
good news that God loves them. Do whatever
you can to spread freedom and vision and
hope. Be a vehicle of the Spirit's grace.

Day 104
A SPECIAL PLACE

My people will live in peaceful places and in
safe homes and in calm places of rest.
ISAIAH 32:18 NCV

Home is the place where you feel the most
comfortable—the place where you can kick off
your shoes, put on your bathrobe, and relax.
God has created this place for you, a place
where His grace can soothe your heart in a
special way.

Day 105
LONGING FOR HOME

This is what the LORD says: "You will be in Babylon for seventy years. But then I will come and do for you all the good things I have promised, and I will bring you home again."

JEREMIAH 29:10 NLT

Sometimes in life we go through periods when we feel out of place, as though we just don't belong. Our hearts feel restless and lonely. We long to go home, but we don't know how. God uses those times to teach us special things we need to know, but He never leaves us in exile. His grace always brings us home.

Day 106
FEAR WILL FLEE

Do not be afraid of sudden terror, nor of
trouble from the wicked when it comes;
for the LORD will be your confidence,
and will keep your foot from being caught.
PROVERBS 3:25–26 NKJV

What do you have to fear with God as your
confidence? He protects you from being
snared like a wild animal by the world's troubles. With His hand over you, no sudden event
or evildoer's plot can destroy you. Give Him
your confidence, and fear will flee.

Day 107
FEARING GOD

In the fear of the LORD there
is strong confidence, and His
children will have a place of refuge.
PROVERBS 14:26 NKJV

There is only one right kind of fear—the fear
of God. Not that we need to cower before Him,
but we must respect and honor Him and His
infinite power. Those who love Him also rightly
fear Him. But those who fear God need fear
nothing else. He is their refuge, the Protector
whom nothing can bypass. Fear God, and you
are safe.

Day 108
WHOM DO YOU FEAR?

"I tell you, my friends, do not be afraid of those who kill the body and after that can do no more."
LUKE 12:4

Whom do you fear? If it's anyone other than God, take heart. You need not concern yourself with anything that person can do to you. Even those who can take your life can't change your eternal destination. So, if someone doesn't like your faith, don't sweat it. Put your trust in God and serve Him faithfully, and you need not fear.

Day 109
FREEDOM FROM FEAR

You came near when I called you,
and you said, "Do not fear."
LAMENTATIONS 3:57

As tentacles of fear attempt to wrap themselves
about us, we struggle to escape. But freedom
lies in our Redeemer. His still, small voice
speaks to our hearts: "Do not fear. What terror
is greater than I?" He who created the universe will never be taken unaware by troubles
or disturbed by our dread. They cannot disrupt
His plan. The future lies clear before His eyes,
and He saves us from every harm.

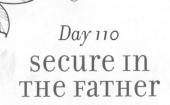

Day 110
secure in the father

The Spirit you received does not make you
slaves, so that you live in fear again; rather, the
Spirit you received brought about your adoption
to sonship. And by him we cry, "Abba, Father."
ROMANS 8:15

As part of God's family, you need never dread
anything. He who rules the universe adopted
you. Since your loving Father no longer con-
demns you for sin, panic need not rule your
life. Fear no retribution, because Jesus shed
His blood for you, covering every sin. God's
child always remains secure in her Abba,
"Daddy."

Day 111
FILLED WITH grace

*"There is plenty of room for you in
my Father's home. If that weren't so,
would I have told you that I'm on my
way to get a room ready for you?"*

JOHN 14:2 MSG

None of us knows exactly what lies on the other
side of death's dark door. But we do know
this: death will take us home. Jesus promised
us that. He wouldn't have said it just to make
us feel better; Jesus wasn't one for telling
polite lies! So, we can trust that right now
He is getting our home in heaven ready for
us, filling it with grace. When we enter the
door, we will find it is exactly right for us, the
place for which we have always longed.

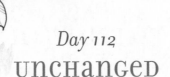

Day 112
UNCHANGED

Why am I discouraged? Why is my
heart so sad? I will put my hope in God!
PSALM 42:5 NLT

Thousands of years ago, the psalmist who
wrote these words expressed the same feelings we all have. Some days we just feel blue.
The world looks dark, everything seems to
be going wrong, and our hearts are sad. Those
feelings are part of the human condition. Like
the psalmist, we need to remind ourselves
that God is unchanged by cloudy skies and
gloomy hearts. His grace is always the same,
as bright and hopeful as ever.

Day 113
AMAZING EXPECTATIONS

Listen to my voice in the morning, Lord.
Each morning I bring my requests
to you and wait expectantly.
PSALM 5:3 NLT

You need to get in the habit of hoping. Instead of getting up in the morning and sighing as you face another dreary day, practice saying hello to God as soon as you wake up. Listen for what He wants to say to your heart. Expect Him to do amazing things each day.

Day 114
AN ATTITUDE

GOD proves to be good to the man who
passionately waits, to the woman who
diligently seeks. It's a good thing to quietly
hope, quietly hope for help from GOD.
LAMENTATIONS 3:25 MSG

Hope is an attitude, not an emotion. It means
putting our whole hearts into relying on God.
It means keeping our eyes focused on Him no
matter what, waiting for Him to reveal Himself
in our lives. God never disappoints those who
passionately wait for His help, who diligently
seek His grace.

Day 115
GRACE OF HOSPITALITY

When God's people are in need,
be ready to help them. Always be
eager to practice hospitality.
ROMANS 12:13 NLT

God opens Himself to you, offering you everything He has, and He calls you to do the same for others. Just as He made you welcome, make others welcome in your life. Don't reach out to others grudgingly, with a sense of obligation. Instead, be eager for opportunities to practice the grace of hospitality.

Day 116
OPEN HOMES

Be quick to give a meal to the hungry,
a bed to the homeless—cheerfully.
1 PETER 4:9 MSG

Because our homes are our private places, the places we retreat to, to find new strength when we're tired, it's hard sometimes to open our homes to others. It's bad enough that we have to cope with others' needs all day long, we feel, without having to bring them home with us! But God calls us to offer our hospitality, and He will give us the grace to do it joyfully.

Day 117
BLESSING OF FORGIVENESS

*[Our] sins have been forgiven
on account of his name.*

1 JOHN 2:12

Who could do something wonderful enough
to earn God's forgiveness? No human work
can buy it. God forgives because of who He
is, not because of who we are or what we do.
That's encouraging because we can't earn
forgiveness by our own perfection. Instead,
forgiveness becomes the great blessing of
our Christian life that makes living for Jesus
possible. We obey God to show our appreciation, not to gain entry into His kingdom.

Day 118

AN END TO
MOURNING

*"Blessed are those who mourn,
for they will be comforted."*

MATTHEW 5:4

How often do we think of mourning as a good thing? But when it comes to sin, it is. Those who sorrow over their own sinfulness will turn to God for forgiveness. When He willingly responds to their repentance, mourning ends. Comforted by God's pardon, transformed sinners celebrate—and joyous love for Jesus replaces sorrow.

Day 119
THE PRICE OF FORGIVENESS

And according to the law almost all things
are purified with blood, and without
shedding of blood there is no remission.
HEBREWS 9:22 NKJV

Many people in our world would like cheap
forgiveness. They want someone to say they are
okay, but they don't want to pay any price for
their wrongdoing. That's not what the scriptures say. Remission of sins comes at a high
price—sacrificial blood, the blood of Jesus.
Jesus says you are worth this expense, and you
are clean in Him. Put sin away and rejoice in
His deep love for you.

Day 120
PASS IT ON

*"If you forgive other people for their offenses,
your heavenly Father will also forgive you."*
MATTHEW 6:14 NASB

Forgiveness isn't something God gives only to
us. He designed it to be passed on to others.
Doing that, we learn the value of the pardon the
Father offered us. Even when everything in us
screams, "No, I can't forgive," He empowers us
to do so if we trust in Him. Our loving Father
never commands us to actions He cannot also
strengthen us to do.

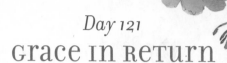

Day 121
Grace in Return

" 'Master, what are you talking about? When did we ever see you hungry and feed you, thirsty and give you a drink? And when did we ever see you sick or in prison and come to you?' Then the King will say, 'I'm telling the solemn truth: Whenever you did one of these things to someone overlooked or ignored, that was me—you did it to me.' "

MATTHEW 25:37–40 MSG

If Christ were at our doorstep, tired and hungry, what would we do? We like to think we would throw the door wide open and welcome Him into our home. Truly, we're given the opportunity to offer hospitality to Jesus each time we're faced with a person in need. His grace reaches out to us through those who feel misunderstood and overlooked, and He wants us to offer that same grace in return.

Day 122
everyone

If your enemy is hungry, feed him.
If he is thirsty, give him a drink.

PROVERBS 25:21 NCV

It's easy to have our friends over for dinner. Offering our hospitality to the people who give us pleasure is not much of a hardship. But hospitality gets harder when we offer it to the people who hurt our feelings, the people we really don't like very much. But God calls us to reach out in practical, tangible ways to *everyone*. Seek His grace to do this in some way every day.

Day 123
THINKING HABITS

*And now, dear brothers and sisters,
one final thing. Fix your thoughts on what
is true, and honorable, and right, and pure,
and lovely, and admirable. Think about
things that are excellent and worthy of praise.*

PHILIPPIANS 4:8 NLT

Our brains are gifts from God, intended to serve us well, special gifts of grace we often take for granted. In return, we need to offer our minds to God. Practice thinking positive thoughts. Focus on what is true rather than on lies. Pay attention to beautiful things, and stop staring at the ugly things in life. Discipline your minds to take on God's habits of thinking.

Day 124
BEYOND INTELLIGENCE

*The fastest runner does not always win the race,
the strongest soldier does not always win the
battle, the wisest does not always have food, the
smartest does not always become wealthy, and
the talented one does not always receive praise.
Time and chance happen to everyone.*

ECCLESIASTES 9:11 NCV

How smart do you think you are? Do you assume you will be able to think your way through life's problems? Many of us do—but God reminds us that some things are beyond the scope of our intelligence. Some days life simply doesn't make sense. But even then, grace is there with us in the chaos. When we can find no rational answers to life's dilemmas, we must rely absolutely on God.

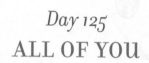

Day 125
ALL OF YOU

*"Love the Lord God with all your passion
and prayer and intelligence and energy."*
MARK 12:30 MSG

God wants all of you. He wants the "spiritual parts," but He also wants your emotions, your physical energy, and your brain's intelligence. Offer them all to God as expressions of your love for Him. Let His grace use every part of you!

Day 126
Brand-New Ways

Intelligent people are always ready to learn.
Their ears are open for knowledge.
PROVERBS 18:15 NLT

Whether or not you did well in school, you probably rely on your intelligence to get you through life. If you're really intelligent, though, you will remember that no matter how many years it has been since you graduated, you are never done learning. You need to be open to new ideas, willing to give up old, stale ways of thinking. When you are, you will find God's grace revealed in brand-new ways.

Day 127
CHOSEN FAMILY

*There is a friend that sticketh
closer than a brother.*
PROVERBS 18:24 KJV

Family relationships range from the wonderful to the disturbing, and we get whatever God gives us. But we choose our friends based on common interests and experiences. Often this "chosen family" seems closer to us than siblings. Yet neither clings closer than our elder brother, Jesus. He teaches us how to love blood relatives and those we choose. It doesn't matter if we're related or not, when we love in Him, that love sticks fast.

Day 128
DISCONNECT FROM THE WORLD

Whosoever therefore will be a friend
of the world is the enemy of God.

JAMES 4:4 KJV

There are good friendships and bad ones.
When Christ becomes your best friend, other
relationships may become distant. Old,
worldly friendships no longer seem so at-
tractive. Your lifestyles clash, and old friends
become confused. But this separation is part
of God's plan of holiness. Jesus disconnects
you from the world and draws you close to
His people—Christian friends who share your
love for Him. Together, you may reach out to
those old friends for Jesus too.

Day 129
Importance of Friendship

Do not forsake your friend and a friend of your family, and do not go to your relative's house when disaster strikes you—better a neighbor nearby than a relative far away.
PROVERBS 27:10

Friendship is important to God, or He would not encourage us to hold fast to it. As Christians, we've known times when other believers seemed closer than our kin. God has brought us into a new family—His own—where faith becomes more important than blood. Through Him, our love expands, and we help each other when trouble strikes. No matter where you go, God's people are near.

Day 130
OUR BEST FRIEND

The righteous choose their friends carefully,
but the way of the wicked leads them astray.

PROVERBS 12:26

We need friends. But there are those who will lead us into trouble and those who will encourage us and lift us up in our faith, drawing us ever nearer to God. Before we draw near to others, do we consider their spiritual impact on us? If God is our best friend, let us be cautious not to be led astray. When we share friendship with Jesus and our earthly friends, we are truly blessed.

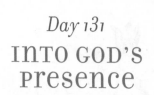

Day 131
INTO GOD'S PRESENCE

*"[When] that person can pray to God
and find favor with him, they will
see God's face and shout for joy."*

Job 33:26

Prayer is the channel through which God's grace flows. We do not pray because God needs us to pray; we pray because *we* need to pray. When we come into God's presence, we are renewed. Our hearts lift. We look into the face of the One who loves us most, and we are filled with joy.

Day 132
ETERNAL JOY

You make known to me the path of life;
you will fill me with joy in your presence,
with eternal pleasures at your right hand.
PSALM 16:11

God does not want you to be unhappy and confused. Believe in His grace. He is waiting to show you the way to go. He is longing to give you the joy of His presence. He wants to make you happy forever.

Day 133
SHINE!

The precepts of the LORD are right,
giving joy to the heart. The commands of
the LORD are radiant, giving light to the eyes.

PSALM 19:8

As children, we probably felt sometimes as
though rules had no purpose but to make us
miserable. We didn't always understand that
our parents' love was behind their rules. As
adults, we often have the same attitude toward
God's rules. We feel as though a life of sin
might be easier, more fun. Instead, it's just the
opposite. God always wants what will give us
joy. His rules are designed to make us shine.

Day 134
WHAT GOD SHOWS US

The LORD is righteous in everything
he does; he is filled with kindness.
PSALM 145:17 NLT

Did you know that the word *kind* comes from
the same root as *kin*? Both words originally
had to do with intimate shared relationships
like the ones that exist between members of
the same family. This is what God shows us:
the kindness of a good father, the gentleness
of a good mother, the understanding of a
brother or sister.

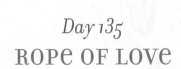

Day 135
ROPE OF LOVE

*"I led them with cords of human kindness,
with ropes of love. I lifted the yoke from
their neck and bent down and fed them."*

HOSEA 11:4 NCV

God's grace is not a lasso looped around our
shoulders, trapping us and binding us tight.
Instead, grace reaches out to us through the
kindness of others. It is a rope of love that
stretches through our lives, leading us to
freedom.

Day 136
FREELY GIVEN

Out of sheer generosity he put us in right
standing with himself. A pure gift. He got
us out of the mess we're in and restored
us to where he always wanted us to be.
And he did it by means of Jesus Christ.
ROMANS 3:24 MSG

How kind God has been to us! He brought us
close to Himself. He reached down and picked
us up out of our messy lives. He healed us so
we could be the people we were always meant
to be. That is what grace is: a gift we never
deserved, freely given out of love.

Day 137
CHOOSE GRACE

And a servant of the Lord must not
quarrel but must be kind to everyone,
a good teacher, and patient.
2 TIMOTHY 2:24 NCV

Some days we can't help but feel irritated and
out of sorts. But no matter how we feel on the
inside, we can choose our outward behavior.
We can make the decision to let disagreements
go, to refuse to argue, to act in kindness, to
show patience and a willingness to listen (even
when we *feel* impatient). We can choose to
walk in grace.

Day 138
LAUGH OUT LOUD

"He will once again fill your mouth with
laughter and your lips with shouts of joy."
JOB 8:21 NLT

Did you know that God wants to make you laugh? He wants to fill you with loud, rowdy joy. Oh, some days His grace will come to you quietly and calmly. But every now and then, you will have days when He makes you laugh out loud.

Day 139
Transformed

And Sarah declared, "God has brought me laughter. All who hear about this will laugh with me."

GENESIS 21:6 NLT

The first time we read of Sarah laughing, it was because she doubted God. She didn't believe that at her age she would have a baby. But God didn't hold her laughter against her. Instead, He transformed it. He turned her laughter of scorn and doubt into the laughter of fulfillment and grace.

Day 140
TRUST HIM

"You people who are now crying are blessed,
because you will laugh with joy."
LUKE 6:21 NCV

God's grace comes to you even in the midst of
tears. He is there with you in your hurt and your
sadness. Trust in Him, knowing that sadness
does not last forever. One day you will laugh
again.

Day 141
WITNESS OF LAUGHTER

We were filled with laughter, and we sang for joy. And the other nations said, "What amazing things the LORD has done for them."

PSALM 126:2 NLT

Life is truly amazing. Each day, grace touches us in many ways, from the sun on our faces to each person we meet, from the love of our friends and families to the satisfaction of our work. Pay attention. Let people hear you laugh more. Don't hide your joy. It's a witness to God's love.

Day 142
FULL!

*I came that they may have and
enjoy life, and have it in abundance
(to the full, till it overflows).*

JOHN 10:10 AMPC

The life we have in Christ is not restricted or
narrow. Grace doesn't flow to us in a mea-
ger trickle; it fills our life to the fullest. God's
grace comes to us each moment, day after
day, year after year, a generous flood that fills
every crack and crevice of our lives—and then
overflows.

Day 143
SING!

But each day the LORD pours his unfailing love upon me, and through each night I sing his songs, praying to God who gives me life.
PSALM 42:8 NLT

Life itself is a gift of grace. The very blood that flows through our veins, the beat of our hearts, and the steady hum of our metabolism—all are God's free gifts to us, tokens of His constant and unconditional love. When we are so richly loved, how can we help but sing, even in the darkness?

Day 144
surrender

"For whoever wants to save their life will lose it,
but whoever loses their life for me will save it."
LUKE 9:24

Life is full of paradoxes. God seems to delight
in turning our ideas inside out and backward.
It doesn't seem to make sense, but the only way
to possess our life is to surrender it absolutely
into God's hands. As we let go of everything,
God's grace gives everything back to us, transformed by His love.

Day 145
RADIANT

"If you are filled with light, with no dark corners, then your whole life will be radiant, as though a floodlight were filling you with light."
LUKE 11:36 NLT

In our lives, we all have dark corners we keep hidden. We hide them from others. We hide them from God, and we even try to hide them from ourselves. But God wants to shine His light even into our darkest, most private nooks and crannies. He wants us to step out into the floodlight of His love—and then His grace will make us shine.

Day 146
PRAYERFUL GIVING

Give, and it shall be given unto you;
good measure, pressed down
. . .and running over.
LUKE 6:38 KJV

Need an example of how to give? Look to God. To those who give generously, He gives over-flowing, abundant blessings. In this fallen world, we need to be careful to whom we give support. Dishonest people or those who oppose God should not be our charitable choices. But many Christian ministries do good work and need our support. Faithful churches need our giving. As we donate prayerfully, God will bless us in return.

Day 147
WANT VS. NEED

"Give us this day our daily bread."
MATTHEW 6:11 NKJV

Jesus tells us here to ask God for our daily
needs, and we may do that frequently. Let's
remember that even the smallest things, such
as the bread we put on the table, come from
God. Yet, have we forgotten that all our food
comes from our heavenly Father? God forgets
nothing we need. So, if we don't have steak
instead of hamburgers, could it be because
we want but don't need it?

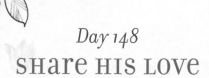

Day 148
SHARE HIS LOVE

*"It is more blessed to
give than to receive."*
ACTS 20:35

Christmas has become a time of receiving—
to the point where greed motivates more people than blessing. But Paul reminds us that
getting what we want is not the greatest blessing. We know that when we see the delight in
a child's eyes at receiving a longed-for item.
Our heavenly Father loves to see the same joy
in our eyes when He helps us in less tangible
ways. That's why He tells us to share His love
with others.

Day 149
GETTING WHAT YOU GIVE

Whoever sows sparingly will also reap sparingly, and whoever sows generously will also reap generously.

2 CORINTHIANS 9:6

What you give is what you get. That's true in life, and it's also true spiritually. Anyone who tries to hold their finances close will be letting go of spiritual blessings, while the person who shares generously gains in so many ways. It's hard to give up worldly treasures, but when you give in the name of Jesus, you will never run short.

Day 150
LOVE IS BIGGER

*"Love the L*ORD *your God with
all your heart and with all your
soul and with all your strength."*
DEUTERONOMY 6:5 NASB

Love is not merely a feeling. It's far bigger
than that. Love fills up our emotions, but it
also fills our thoughts. Our body's strength
and energy feed it. It requires discipline and
determination. Loving God requires the effort
of our whole being.

Day 151
ACT IN LOVE

Let all that you do be done in love.
1 CORINTHIANS 16:14 NRSV

Because love is not merely an emotion, it needs to become real through action. We grow in love as we act in love. Some days the emotion may overwhelm us; other days we may feel nothing at all. But if we express our love while making meals, driving the car, talking to our families, or cleaning the house, God's love will flow through us to the world around us—and we will see His grace at work.

Day 152
WEB OF LOVE

"So now I am giving you a new commandment:
Love each other. Just as I have loved you,
you should love each other."

JOHN 13:34 NLT

God's grace comes to us through a network
of relationships and connections. Because
we know we are totally and unconditionally
loved, we can, in turn, love others. The connections between us grow ever wider and
stronger, a web of love that unites us all
with God.

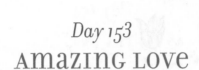

Day 153
Amazing Love

Your unfailing love, O Lord, is as vast
as the heavens; your faithfulness
reaches beyond the clouds.
Psalm 36:5 nlt

God loves you. The Creator of the universe cares about you, and His love is unconditional and limitless. You can never make Him tired of you; He will never abandon you. You are utterly and completely loved, no matter what, forever and ever.

Isn't that amazing?

Day 154
THRIVE!

Those who trust in their riches will fall,
but the righteous will thrive like a green leaf.

PROVERBS 11:28

Money seems so important in our world. Many things we want depend on money—that remodeling project we're hoping to do, the summer clothes we want to buy, the Christmas gifts we want to give, the vacation we hope to take, and the new car we want to drive. There's nothing wrong with any of those things, but our enjoyment of them will always be fleeting. Only God's daily grace makes us truly grow and thrive.

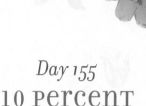

Day 155
10 percent

The earth is the LORD's,
and everything in it.
PSALM 24:1 NLT

Do you tithe? Giving 10 percent of your income specifically to God's work is a good discipline. But sometimes we act as though that 10 percent is God's and the other 90 percent is ours. We forget that *everything* is God's. Through grace, He shares all creation with us. When we look at it that way, our 10 percent tithe seems a little stingy!

Day 156
WHAT YOU NEED

Give me neither poverty nor riches!
Give me just enough to satisfy my needs.
PROVERBS 30:8 NLT

God gives us what we need, and He knows exactly what and how much that is. Whatever He has given you financially, He knows that is what you need right now. Trust His grace. He will satisfy your needs.

Day 157
DEPTH OF GOD'S RICHES

Oh, the depth of the riches of the wisdom and knowledge of God! How unsearchable his judgments, and his paths beyond tracing out!
ROMANS 11:33

Money is the way our culture measures value, but we forget that it's just a symbol, a unit of measurement that can never span the infinite value of God's grace. Imagine trying to use a tape measure to stretch across the galaxy or a teaspoon to determine how much water is in the sea. In the same way, money will always fall short if we use it to try to understand the depth of God's riches.

Day 158
ALL YOU REALLY NEED

Don't wear yourself out trying to get rich;
be wise enough to control yourself.
PROVERBS 23:4 NCV

Some nights we lie awake worrying about bills
that need to be paid. When Sunday comes, we
sit in church preoccupied with how we can
afford to pay for a new car, our kids' college
bills, or the taxes. We think about the things
we would like to buy. And then we work harder
and harder to earn the money we think we
have to have. When you catch yourself doing
that—stop! God's grace is all you really need.

Day 159
LOVING CORRECTION

For whom the LORD loves He corrects,
just as a father the son in whom he delights.
PROVERBS 3:12 NKJV

Do you feel the pain of God's correction? Take heart, since it shows He loves you. Just as a loving father will not let his child walk in a dangerous place, your heavenly Father is redirecting you onto another path. Today's discipline may hurt, but in days to come, your sorrow will turn to joy as you reap the blessing that follows obedience. Your Father loves you deeply.

Day 160
compassion

A father to the fatherless, a defender
of widows, is God in his holy dwelling.
Psalm 68:5

God's love is very tender toward those who
hurt. Children who have lost their fathers and
women who have lost their husbands can count
on His compassion. When we lose a loved one,
do we focus on the Father's gentleness? We
are more likely to complain that He did not
extend life than to praise Him for His care. But
when we feel the most pain, we also receive the
largest portion of God's comfort. What hurts
His children hurts Him too.

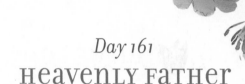

Day 161
HEAVENLY FATHER

The mighty God, The everlasting Father. . .
ISAIAH 9:6 KJV

If you have accepted Jesus as your Savior, God is always your Father. Distance, disagreement, or death cannot change that, though each may separate you from your earthly father. But a human parent is neither mighty nor everlasting and may fail physically or spiritually. Only your heavenly Father will always be there for you, guiding you every step of the way. When you need help, call on your Father; He will never fail.

Day 162
CHILDREN OF GOD

*Because you are his sons, God sent
the Spirit of his Son into our hearts,
the Spirit who calls out, "Abba, Father."*
GALATIANS 4:6

God draws His children near, connecting them firmly to Himself through the Son and the Holy Spirit. There is no division in the Godhead when it comes to loving God's adopted children. With the Spirit, we call out, "Abba, Daddy," to the Holy One who loved us enough to call us to Himself, despite our sin. Through Jesus' sacrifice and the Spirit's work, God the Father cleanses us and opens communications so we can follow Him truly.

Day 163
HE LOVES YOU THIS MUCH!

See what great love the Father has lavished
on us, that we should be called children
of God! And that is what we are!

1 JOHN 3:1

God does not give His love in dribs and drabs.
He lavishes it on us when we come to Him in
faith. All along, He was waiting to make us
His children, and we were the ones who re-
sisted. But once we face Him as His children,
God's love lets loose in our lives. Nothing is
too good for His obedient children. Praise
God that He loves you that much!

Day 164

TURN TO HIM

"I will be a Father to you, and you shall be My sons and daughters, says the LORD Almighty."

2 CORINTHIANS 6:18 NKJV

Only unconfessed sin can separate you from the Father. But God never desires such distance. He wants to draw near, like a loving Father who holds His child, provides for her, and helps her at every turn. Though your earthly father was less than perfect, your heavenly Father is not. He heals your hurts, solves your problems, and offers His love at every turn. All you need to do is turn to Him in love.

Day 165
SHARING LIFE

But if we walk in the light, God himself
being the light, we also experience
a shared life with one another.

1 JOHN 1:7 MSG

Some of us are extroverts, and some of us are
introverts. But either way, God asks us to share
our lives in some way with others. As we walk
in His light, He gives us grace to experience
a new kind of a life, a life we have in common with the others who share His kingdom.

Day 166
LOVING SUPPORT

*Let us think of ways to motivate one
another to acts of love and good works.*
HEBREWS 10:24 NLT

Imagine that you're sitting in the bleachers
watching one of your favorite young people
play a sport. You jump up and cheer for him.
You make sure he knows you're there, shout-
ing out encouragement. Hearing your voice,
he jumps higher, runs faster. That is the sort
of excitement and support we need to show
others around us. When we do all we can to
encourage each other, love and good deeds
will burst from us all.

Day 167
CHRIST FOLLOWERS

"This is what the LORD All-Powerful says:
'Do what is right and true. Be kind
and merciful to each other.'"
ZECHARIAH 7:9 NCV

As Christ's followers, we need to interact with others the way He did when He was on earth. That means we don't lie to each other, and we don't use others. Instead, we practice kindness and mercy. We let God's grace speak through our mouths.

Day 168

OVERFLOWING LOVE

*And may the Lord make your love for
one another and for all people grow and
overflow, just as our love for you overflows.*
1 THESSALONIANS 3:12 NLT

As a very young child, you thought you were
the center of the world. As you grew older,
you had to go through the painful process of
learning that others' feelings were as important as yours. God's grace wants to lift your
perspective even higher, though. He wants you
to overflow with love for other people.

Day 169
HEALED PAST

*"All their past sins will be forgotten,
and they will live because of the
righteous things they have done."*

EZEKIEL 18:22 NLT

We have the feeling that we can't do anything
about the past. We think all our mistakes are
back there behind us, carved in stone. But
God's creative power is amazing, and His grace
can heal even the past. Yesterday's sins are
pulled out like weeds, while the good things
we have done are watered so that they grow
and flourish into the present. Give your past
to God. His grace is big enough to bring healing even to your worst memories.

Day 170
LOOKING FORWARD

I focus on this one thing: Forgetting the past
and looking forward to what lies ahead.
PHILIPPIANS 3:13 NLT

As followers of Christ, we are people who look
forward rather than backward. We have all
made mistakes, but God does not want us to
dwell on them, wallowing in guilt and discouragement. Instead, He calls us to let go of the
past, trusting Him to deal with it. His grace is
new every moment.

Day 171
RENEWAL

*"Look, the winter is past,
and the rains are over and gone."*
SONG OF SOLOMON 2:11 NLT

Dreary times of cold and rain come to us all. Just as the earth needs those times to renew itself, so do we. As painful as those times are, grace works through them to make us into the people God has called us to be. But once those times are over, there's no need to continue to dwell on them. Go outside and enjoy the sunshine!

Day 172
YOU WILL LIVE

*Their past sins will be forgiven,
and they will live.*
EZEKIEL 33:16 CEV

Do you ever feel doomed? Do you feel as though your mistakes are waiting to fall on your head, like a huge rock that will crush the life out of you? We all have moments like that. But God's grace doesn't let that enormous boulder drop. His forgiveness catches it and rolls it away. You will live after all!

Day 173
valuable

Better to be patient than powerful;
better to have self-control
than to conquer a city.
PROVERBS 16:32 NLT

Our world values visible power. We appreciate things like prestige and skill, wealth and influence. But God looks at things differently. From His perspective, the quiet, easily overlooked quality of patience is far more valuable than any worldly power. Patience makes room for others' needs and brokenness. Patience creates a space in our lives for God's grace to flow through us.

Day 174
QUIET TIME

Be still before the LORD,
and wait patiently for him.
PSALM 37:7 NRSV

Our lives are busy. Responsibilities crowd our days, and at night as we go to bed, our minds often continue to be preoccupied with the day's work, ticking off a mental to-do list even as we fall asleep. We need to set aside time to quiet our hearts. In those moments, we can let go of all our to-dos and wait for God's grace to act in our lives.

Day 175
QUIET GRACE

Patient persistence pierces through indifference;
gentle speech breaks down rigid defenses.
PROVERBS 25:15 MSG

When we're in the midst of an argument, we often become fixated on winning. We turn conflicts into power struggles, and we want to come out the victor. By sheer force, if necessary, we want to shape people to our will. But that is not the way God treats us. His grace is gentle and patient rather than loud and forceful. We need to follow His example and let His quiet grace speak through us in His timing rather than ours.

Day 176
ANOTHER MOMENT LONGER

Wait patiently for the Lord. Be brave and courageous. Yes, wait patiently for the Lord.
PSALM 27:14 NLT

Patience is all about waiting things out. It's about holding on another moment longer. It means enduring hard times. As a younger person, you probably felt you couldn't possibly endure certain things, but the older you get, the more you realize that you can. If you just wait long enough, the tide always turns. Hold on. Your life will change. God's grace will rescue you.

Day 177
STAND FIRM

The LORD has become my fortress,
and my God the rock in whom I take refuge.
PSALM 94:22

Are you under attack by friends, family, or coworkers? If it comes because of your obedience to the Lord, stand firm in the face of their comments. He will defend you. If you face harsh words or nasty attitudes, remain kind, and He will assist you. Should your boss do you wrong, don't worry. Those who are against a faithful Christian are also against Him, and God will somehow make things right.

Day 178
OUR REFUGE

"The LORD Almighty is the one you are to regard as holy. . . . He will be a holy place."
ISAIAH 8:13–14

When you live in awe of God—when He alone is Lord of your life—you have nothing to fear. If fears or enemies assail you, a place of refuge is always nearby. God never throws His children to the wolves. Instead, He protects them in His holy place. With Jesus as your Savior, you always have a peaceful place to go to.

Day 179
RECEIVE HIS STRENGTH

*The Lord also will be a refuge for the
oppressed, a refuge in times of trouble.*
PSALM 9:9 NKJV

The psalms often speak of God as a refuge.
Whether you face something large, like op-
pression, or something much smaller, He
wants you to turn to Him in troubled times.
Size does not matter, but your trust in Jesus
does. Nothing you face is a shock to Him—
He knows your troubles and has not deserted
you. So, go to your refuge and take strength
from Him.

Day 180
NOTHING IS HIDDEN

*Nothing in all creation is
hidden from God's sight.*
HEBREWS 4:13

Good or bad, nothing escapes God's notice.
None of it is unknown to the Creator of the
universe. And because He knows all, we can
completely trust in God. He protects us from
the wicked and supports the good in our lives
because He knows just how both will touch us.
When sorrow or trouble comes our way, we
can count on His using it to benefit us—here
and in eternity.

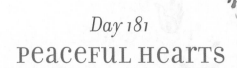

Day 181
PEACEFUL HEARTS

You will keep in perfect peace all who trust in you, all whose thoughts are fixed on you!
ISAIAH 26:3 NLT

Peace seems very far away sometimes. But it's not! Peace isn't an emotion we can work up in our own strength. It's one of the gifts of grace God longs to give us. All we need to do is focus on Him. As we give Him all our worries, one by one, every day, He will do His part: He will keep our hearts at peace.

Day 182
PEACE RULES

And let the peace that comes from Christ
rule in your hearts. For as members of
one body you are called to live in peace.
COLOSSIANS 3:15 NLT

Peace is a way of living our lives. It happens when we let Christ's peace into our lives to rule over our emotions, our doubts, and our worries, and then go one step more and let His peace control the way we live. Peace is God's gift of grace to us, but it is also the way to a graceful life, the path to harmony with the world around us.

Day 183
AN ALL-THE-TIME THING!

Pray diligently. Stay alert,
with your eyes wide open in gratitude.
COLOSSIANS 4:2 MSG

Prayer is not a sometimes thing. It's an all-the-time thing! We need to pray every day, being careful to keep the lines of communication open between God and ourselves all through the day, moment by moment. When we make prayer a habit, we won't miss the many gifts of grace that come our way. And we won't forget to notice when God answers our prayers.

Day 184

THE CENTER
OF OUR LIVES

*The apostles often met together and
prayed with a single purpose in mind.*
ACTS 1:14 CEV

What do you do when you get together with
the people you're close to? You probably talk
and laugh, share a meal, maybe go shopping,
or work on a project. But do you ever pray together? If prayer is the center of our lives, we
will want to share this gift of grace with those
with whom we're closest.

Day 185

ALONE TIME
WITH GOD

*But Jesus often withdrew to
the wilderness for prayer.*
LUKE 5:16 NLT

God is always with us, even when we're too
busy to do more than whisper a prayer in the
shower or as we drive the car. But if even Jesus
needed to make time to get away by Himself
for some alone time with God, then we certainly need to do so as well. In those quiet moments of prayer by ourselves with God, we will
find the grace we need to live our busy lives.

Day 186
HE'S WAITING. . .

"The eyes of the LORD watch over those who do right, and his ears are open to their prayers."
1 PETER 3:12 NLT

You don't have to try to get God's attention. He is watching you right now. His ear is tuned to your voice. All you need to do is speak, and He will hear you. Receive the gift of grace He gives to you through prayer. Tell God your thoughts, your feelings, your hopes, your joys. He's waiting to listen to you.

Day 187
RIGHT NOW

For God says, "At just the right time,
I heard you. On the day of salvation,
I helped you." Indeed, the "right time"
is now. Today is the day of salvation.
2 CORINTHIANS 6:2 NLT

God always meets us right now, in the present moment. We don't need to waste our time looking over our shoulders at the past, and we don't have to feel as though we need to reach some future moment before we can truly touch God. He is here now. Today, this very moment, is full of His grace.

Day 188
see jesus

God left nothing that is not subject to them.
Yet at present we do not see everything
subject to them. But we do see Jesus.
HEBREWS 2:8–9

We know that Jesus has won the victory over
sin; yet when we look at the world as it is right
now, we still see sin all around us. We see pain
and suffering, greed and selfishness, brokenness and despair. We know that the world is
not ruled by God. Yet despite that, we can look
past the darkness of sin. By grace, right now,
we can see Jesus.

Day 189
constant grace

For Jesus doesn't change—yesterday, today,
tomorrow, he's always totally himself.
HEBREWS 13:8 MSG

As human beings, we live in the stream of time.
Sometimes all the changes time brings terrify
us; sometimes they fill us with joy and excitement. Either way, we can cling to the still point
that lies in the middle of our changing world:
Jesus Christ, who never changes. His constant
grace leads us through all life's changes, and
one day it will bring us to our home in heaven,
beyond time, where we will be like Him.

Day 190

THE PRESENT MOMENT

"This day is holy to our Lord."
NEHEMIAH 8:10

Sometimes we're in such a hurry to get to the future that we miss out on the present. God has gifts He wants to give you right now. Don't be so excited about tomorrow that you overlook the grace He's giving you today.

Day 191
TODAY'S OPPORTUNITIES

*But encourage each other every day while it is
"today." Help each other so none of you will
become hardened because sin has tricked you.*

HEBREWS 3:13 NCV

Don't put off helping others. Sin tricks us into
thinking we can do it later. But grace doesn't
procrastinate. Take advantage of the opportunities that come your way today.

Day 192
ALWAYS FAITHFUL

I will never leave thee, nor forsake thee.
HEBREWS 13:5 KJV

Even when fear or stress challenges you, you need never deal with it single-handedly if Jesus rules your life. When your life seems in shambles around you, He offers strength and comfort for a hurting heart. God never gives up on you. His love cannot change. Today, delight in the One who never deserts you.

Day 193
NOTHING IS IMPOSSIBLE

"For nothing will be impossible with God."
LUKE 1:37 NRSV

The angel spoke these words to Mary as he gave her the news that the aged Elizabeth would bear a child. God deals with the impossible in our lives too. We do not bear a Savior, but how has He helped us understand impossible relationships, juggle a hectic schedule, or help a hurting friend? God offers aid, whatever we face. Nothing is impossible for the One at work in our lives. What impossibilities can He deal with in your life? Have you trusted Him for help?

Day 194
HE IS FAITHFUL

Blessed are those whose help is the God of Jacob. . .he remains faithful forever.
PSALM 146:5–6

You are not the only one who has experienced God's faithfulness. Through the years, believers have experienced His provision. Read Old Testament accounts of those who have never seen Him fail. Watch His acts in the New Testament as He showed the church that it could trust Him. God cannot fail His children, and He will not fail you. Trust in the God of Jacob, and pass on your testimony of His faithfulness.

Day 195
GOD OFFERS HOPE

"For I know the plans I have for you," declares the LORD, "plans to prosper you and not to harm you, plans to give you hope and a future."

JEREMIAH 29:11

As Judah headed into exile, conquered by a savage pagan people, God offered them hope. He still had a good plan for them, one that would come out of suffering. Their prosperity was not at an end, though their path through hardship had begun.

When God leads you up a rocky path, your hope and future remain secure in Him. Faithful trust is all He asks of you.

Day 196
CALL ON HIM

Our help is in the name of the LORD,
the Maker of heaven and earth.
PSALM 124:8

The name God told to Moses, "I AM WHO I AM," describes His unchanging nature. So here, when the Unchanging One promises to help us, that assurance never alters. What in heaven or on earth could be too powerful or too much trouble for its Maker? Nothing is greater than God, not even our biggest challenge. We need only call His name.

Day 197
ALL-POWERFUL

God is our refuge and strength,
an ever-present help in trouble.

PSALM 46:1

When we face serious troubles, people often
cannot provide the solution. Limited by human
frailty, even the most generous of them
can help us only so much. In every trouble,
we have a greater asset if we believe in Jesus.
Our all-powerful Creator offers protection
from harm and strength for the longest
trial. He always wants to come to our aid. Facing
a trouble of any size? Turn to Him today.

Day 198
never forgotten

Who is like the LORD our God. . .
who stoops down to look on the
heavens and the earth?
PSALM 113:5–6

This all-powerful Lord, to whom the heavens
and earth are small, cares not just for your
universe but for you. The verses that follow
these describe His love for even the most
humble person. Though you may face times of
struggle, your awesome Lord will never forget
you. One day, as verse 8 of this psalm promises,
even the humble can sit with princes.

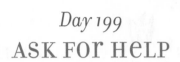

Day 199
ASK FOR HELP

*Let us then approach God's throne of grace with
confidence, so that we may receive mercy and
find grace to help us in our time of need.*
HEBREWS 4:16

Don't feel shy about approaching Jesus with all
your cares. As God's child, you have a special
place in His heart. When you have failed, you
need not fear coming to the King of kings for
mercy and grace. He is just waiting for you
to admit the problem and ask for help. Seek
Jesus' aid, whatever your trouble. That's what
He wants you to do.

Day 200

PURPOSEFUL PLAN

*And we know that all things work together
for good to those who love God, to those who
are the called according to His purpose.*

ROMANS 8:28 NKJV

Life doesn't always look ideal to us. When finances are tight, family problems are serious, or things just don't go our way, we may doubt that God is working in our lives. That's when we need to reread this verse and take heart. Even things that don't seem good have a purpose in God's plan. As Christians, we can trust in Him, even when life is less than perfect.

Day 201
A QUIET PACE

"Teach me, and I will be quiet.
Show me where I have been wrong."
JOB 6:24 NCV

Do you ever feel as though you simply can't
sit still? Your thoughts are swirling so fast
that you can't stop them? You're so busy, so
stressed, so hurried that you have to run, run,
run? Take a breath. Open your heart to God.
Allow Him to quiet your frantic mind. Ask
Him to show you how you can begin again, this
time walking to the quiet pace of His grace.

Day 202
RELAX. . .

But I am calm and quiet, like a baby
with its mother. I am at peace,
like a baby with its mother.
PSALM 131:2 NCV

You know how a baby lies completely limp
in her mother's arms, totally trusting and at
peace? That is the attitude you need to practice.
Let yourself relax in God's arms, wrapped in
His grace. Life will go on around you, with
all its noise and turmoil. Meanwhile, you are
completely safe, totally secure, without a worry
in the world. Lie back and enjoy the quiet!

Day 203
NEW STRENGTH

*"In quietness and confidence
is your strength."*
ISAIAH 30:15 NLT

The weaker we feel, the more we fret. The more
we fret, the weaker we feel. It's a vicious circle.
Stop the circle! Find a quiet place, if only for
a few moments, to draw close to God. Grace
will come to you through the quiet, and you
will discover new strength.

Day 204
NEAR AT HAND

Quiet down before GOD,
be prayerful before him.
PSALM 37:7 MSG

It's not easy to be quiet. Our world is loud, and
the noise seeps into our hearts and minds. We
feel restless and jumpy, on edge. God seems
far away. But God is always near at hand, no
matter how we feel. When we quiet our hearts,
we will find Him there, patiently waiting, ready
to show us His grace.

Day 205
BECAUSE OF CHRIST

All this comes from the God who settled
the relationship between us and him,
and then called us to settle our
relationships with each other.
2 CORINTHIANS 5:18 MSG

God created a bridge to span the distance
between ourselves and Him. That bridge
is Christ, the best and fullest expression of
divine grace. Because of Christ, we are in a
relationship with the Creator of the entire
world. And because of Christ, we are called to
build bridges of our own, to span the distance
between ourselves and others.

Day 206
ALL EQUAL—
BY Grace

Live in peace with each other.
Do not be proud, but make friends
with those who seem unimportant.
Do not think how smart you are.
ROMANS 12:16 NCV

Sometimes other people just seem so stupid! We pride ourselves that *we* would never act like that, dress like that, talk like that. But God wants us to let go of our pride. He wants us to remember that in His eyes we are all equal, all loved, all saved only by grace.

Day 207
ONLY BY GRACE

*Accept one another, then, just as Christ
accepted you, in order to bring praise to God.*
ROMANS 15:7

It's easy to pick out others' faults. Sometimes you may even feel justified in doing so, as though God would approve of your righteousness as you point out others' sinfulness.

Don't forget that Christ accepted you, with all your brokenness and faults. Only by grace were you made whole. Share that grace—that acceptance and unconditional love—with the people around you.

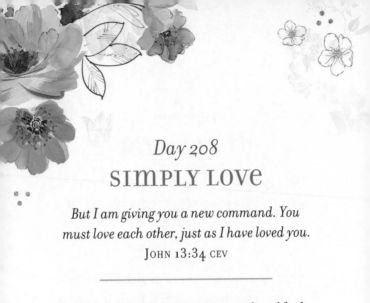

Day 208
SIMPLY LOVE

But I am giving you a new command. You must love each other, just as I have loved you.
JOHN 13:34 CEV

Christ doesn't ask us to point out others' faults. He doesn't require that we be the morality squad, focusing on all that is sinful in the world around us. Instead, He wants us to simply love just as He loves us. When we do, the world will see God's grace shining in our lives.

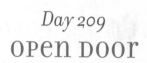

Day 209
open door

For God so loved the world that he gave his one and only Son, that whoever believes in him shall not perish but have eternal life.
JOHN 3:16

These words are God's open door to those who believe in His Son. The barrier between God's holiness and man's sinfulness disintegrates when we believe in Jesus' sacrifice for human sin. But we must walk through that open door, with faith, to inherit the eternal life God offers. Have you taken that step, or are you still outside the door?

Day 210
TENDER LOVE

This is love: not that we loved God,
but that he loved us and sent his Son
as an atoning sacrifice for our sins.

1 JOHN 4:10

We weren't sitting around thinking about loving God before He touched our lives. God began the process before we were even born. He sent His Son to bring us into communion with Him, and His Spirit drew us into a relationship with Him. We respond to God's overwhelmingly tender love when we invite Jesus into our lives. Even so, many years of obedience show our gratitude, but they never repay His loving compassion.

Day 211
GIFT OF LOVE

The LORD takes delight in his people.
PSALM 149:4

God doesn't just like you—He delights in you. You are so special to Him; He brought you into His salvation so He could spend eternity with you. God loves each of His children in a special way. You aren't just another in a long line of His people. He knows every bit of you, your faithfulness and failures, and loves each part of you "to pieces." We could never earn such love—it is His special gift to each of us. Let's rejoice in that blessing today.

Day 212
GOD'S LOVE
IS AT WORK

We have known and believed the love that God
has for us. God is love, and he who abides
in love abides in God, and God in him.

1 JOHN 4:16 NKJV

Trusting in Jesus, you have felt God's love at
work in your inner being. The vibrant connec-
tion that only Christians experience becomes
the center of your life. If you are faithful, His
eternal life renews you from head to toe and
shines forth vibrantly. Your Spirit-inspired
words and actions truly portray God's love to
the world.

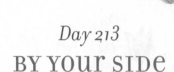

Day 213
BY YOUR SIDE

*Love is patient, love is kind. It does not
envy, it does not boast, it is not proud.*

1 CORINTHIANS 13:4

God's love is not short-tempered or short-
lived. Unlike human love, it never gives up
on you, even on those long, discouraging
days when your job is a strain, family life becomes confused, and you hardly know where
to turn. In such stressful times, your heavenly
Father puts up with all of it, right beside you.
He's not out there somewhere—He's close by
your side.

Day 214

APPRECIATION FOR MERCY

The LORD your God is a merciful God;
he will not abandon or destroy you.
DEUTERONOMY 4:31

Even when we fail God, He does not fail us. He knows our frailty and has mercy when we come to Him seeking forgiveness and wanting to change our ways. Mercy never holds grudges or seeks revenge, but it wants the best for forgiven sinners. So, our merciful Lord calls us to make changes that show we appreciate what He has done for us. Is some appreciation called for in your life?

Day 215
ENDURANCE

As you know, we count as blessed those
who have persevered. You have heard of
Job's perseverance and have seen what the
Lord finally brought about. The Lord is
full of compassion and mercy.

JAMES 5:11

Endurance in faith, hard as it may seem, brings happiness. Trials are not a sign of God's disfavor or His will to carelessly punish His children. The tenderhearted Savior never acts cruelly. But through troubles, we draw close to Him and see God's power at work in our lives. Then, like Job, when we persevere in faith, God rewards us bountifully.

Day 216
MERCY TRIUMPHS

Mercy triumphs over judgment.
JAMES 2:13

Not only is God merciful to us, He expects us to pass that blessing on to others. Instead of becoming the rule enforcers in this world, He wants us to paint a picture of the tender love He has for fallen people and to call many other sinners into His love. When we criticize the world and do not show compassion, we lose the powerful witness we were meant to have. As you stand firm for Jesus, may mercy also triumph in your life.

Day 217
REBIRTH AND RENEWAL

He saved us, not because of righteous
things we had done, but because of his
mercy. He saved us through the washing
of rebirth and renewal by the Holy Spirit.
TITUS 3:5

Could we save ourselves? No way! Even our
best efforts fall far short of God's perfection.
If God had left us on our own, we'd be eter-
nally separated from Him. But graciously,
the Father reached down to us through His
Son, sacrificing Jesus on the cross. Then the
Spirit touched our lives in rebirth and renewal.
Together, the three Persons of the Godhead
saved us in merciful love.

Day 218

JOY IN OUR TROUBLES

Great is your love, reaching to the heavens;
your faithfulness reaches to the skies.

PSALM 57:10

Has God's mercy touched your life so deeply that you wanted to shout His praises to the skies? That's how the psalmist felt as he trusted in God, despite his troubles. When we look to God in our troubles, our burdened hearts can still find joy. Though we are small and weak, He is most powerful. His strength will overcome our deepest problems, if only we let it.

Day 219
OVERFLOWING MERCY

Israel, put your hope in the LORD,
for with the LORD is unfailing love
and with him is full redemption.
PSALM 130:7

Why hope in God even in dire situations? Because every one of His people greatly needs His overflowing mercy. Our lives are frail, but He is not. Jesus brings the redemption we require. No matter what we face, Jesus walks with us. We need only trust faithfully that His salvation is on the way.

Day 220
FROM THE INSIDE OUT

*Take on an entirely new way of life—a
God-fashioned life, a life renewed from the
inside and working itself into your conduct as
God accurately reproduces his character in you.*
EPHESIANS 4:24 MSG

At the end of a long week, we sometimes feel
tired and drained, as though all our creativity
and energy have been robbed from us. We
need to use feelings like that as wake-up calls,
reminders that we need to open ourselves
anew to God's Spirit so that He can renew us
from the inside out. Grace has the power to
change our hearts and minds, filling us with
new energy to follow Jesus.

Day 221
move on

*Anyone who belongs to Christ has
become a new person. The old life
is gone; a new life has begun!*
2 CORINTHIANS 5:17 NLT

You are a brand-new person in Jesus! Don't
worry about what came before. Don't linger
over your guilt and regret. Move on. Step
out into the new, grace-filled life Christ has
given you.

Day 222
Fresh Hearts

"I will give you a new heart and
put a new spirit within you."
EZEKIEL 36:26 NKJV

Life is full of irritations and hassles. Bills to
pay, chores to run, arguments to settle, and
endless responsibilities all stress our hearts
until we feel old and worn. But God renews us.
Day after day, over and over, His grace comes
to us, making our hearts fresh and green and
growing.

Day 223

DRAWING BACK
THE CURTAINS

*But whenever someone turns to the Lord,
the veil is taken away. . . . So all of us who
have had that veil removed can see and reflect
the glory of the Lord. And the Lord—who is the
Spirit—makes us more and more like him as
we are changed into his glorious image.*

2 CORINTHIANS 3:16, 18 NLT

Sometimes we feel as though a thick dark curtain hangs between us and God, hiding Him from our sight. But the Bible says that we just need to turn our hearts to the Lord and the curtain will be drawn back, letting God's glory and grace shine into our lives. When that happens, we can soak up the light, allowing it to renew our hearts and minds into the image of Christ.

Day 224

GOD MEETS OUR NEEDS

"He has brought down rulers from their thrones but has lifted up the humble. He has filled the hungry with good things but has sent the rich away empty."

LUKE 1:52–53

God provides for every one of His children, even the most humble. Wealth cannot gain His favor nor poverty destroy it. The Father does not look at the pocketbook, but at the heart. Those who love Him, though they may lack cash, see their needs fulfilled; but unbelievers who own overflowing storehouses harvest empty hearts. God never ignores His children's needs. What has He given you today?

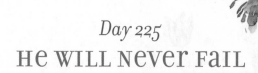

Day 225
HE WILL NEVER FAIL

You open your hand and satisfy
the desires of every living thing.
PSALM 145:16

Our faithful Lord provides for all His created
beings. Will He fail to care for you? How
could He satisfy the needs of the smallest
birds and beasts yet forget His human child?
God is always faithful. Though we fail, He
will not. He cannot forget His promises of
love and will never forget to provide for your
every need.

Day 226
HIS GIFTS

*If, by the trespass of the one man,
death reigned through that one man,
how much more will those who receive
God's abundant provision of grace and
of the gift of righteousness reign in life
through the one man, Jesus Christ.*
ROMANS 5:17

What greater gift could God give us than His
grace? Once, death ruled over us. Now, life
in Christ commands our days. As we ponder
God's compassion, do we appreciate Christ's
sacrifice? Any spiritual value we have comes
from His gifts. We can never repay Him, but
are we living to show how much we care?

Day 227
TRUST GOD

Abraham answered, "God himself will provide the lamb for the burnt offering, my son."
GENESIS 22:8

Though God had commanded Abraham to sacrifice his son, Isaac, the patriarch had faith his son would not die. All it took was a ram caught in a bush. Because of Abraham's faith, the sheep was just where he needed it at the right moment. God provided just what was necessary—a sacrifice and a living son. Do you need God's provision today? Trust the God who made a way for Abraham to make a way for you too.

Day 228
LET HIS LIGHT SHINE

For Christ's sake, I delight in weaknesses,
in insults, in hardships, in persecutions,
in difficulties. For when I am
weak, then I am strong.

2 CORINTHIANS 12:10

Only God can make you strong in the weak places. In those spots of persecution and hardship, His power and grace shine through your fragile vessel as you live as a faithful Christian. When you feel broken and useless, trust in Him to fill your flaws, and His light will shine through the cracks of your pain and reach a hurting world.

Day 229
THE LIVING WORD

The word of God is living and active,
and sharper than any two-edged
sword, even penetrating as far as
the division of soul and spirit.
HEBREWS 4:12 NASB

The Bible is not a dead book. The writer of Hebrews says it lives, and those who trust in Jesus can attest to this truth. Have you read a scripture and felt God knew just what you required because it related to your needs in a special way? Then you've experienced the living Word of God that pierces your soul and spirit. Live by it, in His love.

Day 230

KNOWING GOD

In the beginning was the Word,
and the Word was with God,
and the Word was God.

JOHN 1:1

Want a picture of God's Word? Look at Jesus, the embodiment of everything the Father wanted to say to us. You can't do that if you don't read the Book that tells of Him.

Maybe that's why God takes it personally when we decide not to read His Word. We're ignoring His tender commands and pushing aside His love. God's scriptures communicate with His children. How can we know Him without His Word?

Day 231
FLAWLESS WORDS

"Every word of God is flawless."
PROVERBS 30:5

Maybe you've had days when you've been tempted to doubt this verse. You wanted to go in one direction, and God's Word said to go in another. If you were wise, you trusted in its truth instead of going your own way. After all, can you claim that your every word is error-free? No. How much better to follow in the perfect way of your Lord, who willingly shares His wisdom. To avoid many of the faults of this world, trust the flawless Word of God.

Day 232

COMMITMENT
AND ACTION

Now by this we know that we know Him,
if we keep His commandments.
1 JOHN 2:3 NKJV

How do you know you are a Christian? By the
way you follow your Lord's commandments.
Salvation is not just a matter of feeling His
touch in your life. Faith is not simply a matter of emotion; it requires commitment and
action too. Real love for God contains a passion for following Him. Love Him, and your
life serves Him too.

Day 233
LIVING
CONSISTENTLY

*Then Jesus said to those Jews who
believed Him, "If you abide in My
word, you are My disciples indeed."*
JOHN 8:31 NKJV

Here, Jesus talks to His disciples about a
habitual lifestyle. He wanted them to live
consistently in the truth He had taught them,
not pull His Word out once a week or live by
it once in a while. But this verse isn't only
for those who walked with Jesus during His
earthly ministry. Today, His Spirit helps us
live consistently for Him. As we connect
with the scriptures and obey His commands,
we become disciples too.

Day 234
SAFE IN HIS WILL

*Your hand will guide me,
your right hand will hold me fast.*
PSALM 139:10

Need to make a life-changing decision? God
wants to be part of it. As the psalmist understood, allowing Him to guide your steps means
you won't get off track and land in a nasty situation. For the believer, the best place to be
is in the palm of God's hand, safe from harm
and in the center of His will.

Day 235
EVERY STEP
OF THE WAY

He will be our guide even to the end.
PSALM 48:14

When we are facing dire troubles, God never
deserts us. As life ebbs away, He does not
step back from our need. No, the Eternal One
guides us every step of the way, whether life
is joyous or discouraging. God never gives
up on you and never fails you, so don't give
up on yourself. When times are hard, grab on
to Him more firmly. He will never leave you
nor forsake you. And in the end, you will step
into His arms in heaven.

Day 236
YOU CAN'T
GO WRONG

"In your unfailing love you will lead the people you have redeemed. In your strength you will guide them to your holy dwelling."
EXODUS 15:13

By following Jesus, you always head in the right direction. Though the way may seem dark or convoluted, and you may often wonder if you're on the right track, as His Spirit leads you, you cannot go wrong. Your powerful Lord directs you in His everlasting way. If you start to go wrong, He will guide your steps. God's love never deserts His obedient child.

Day 237
THE LIGHT

When Jesus spoke again to the people,
he said, "I am the light of the world.
Whoever follows me will never walk in
darkness, but will have the light of life."
JOHN 8:12

Following the light of the world means you can see where you're headed. Even when life becomes confusing and totally dark, your goal hasn't changed, and you keep heading in the right direction. Walking in Jesus' light, though you hit a dark patch, you remain on he road with the Savior; and in Him, you always see enough to take the next step.

Day 238
HOPE IN HIM

*Put your hope in God, for I will yet
praise him, my Savior and my God.*
PSALM 42:5

Where else should the believer place her hope?
No human has power to turn her life around
without Jesus. No solution lies beyond Him,
and He never pushes her away. When the world
becomes harsh, she still receives His gentle
encouragement. Though you wait long and
the path seems hard, hold on to Jesus. Words
of praise will pass your lips as you see His
salvation accomplished. Your God will never
let you fall.

Day 239
OVERFLOW
WITH HOPE

*May the God of hope fill you with
all joy and peace as you trust in him,
so that you may overflow with hope
by the power of the Holy Spirit.*

ROMANS 15:13

Where does hope come from? From God.
Unbelievers may have moments of wishful
thinking or snatches of optimism in their
lives, but they cannot exist in an abiding
hope. Christians, filled with the Spirit, see
hope overflow as they live in Christ, fulfilling
the will of the Father. Have faith? Then you
have every reason to hope each day.

Day 240
BE STRONG

Be strong and take heart,
all you who hope in the LORD.
PSALM 31:24

Hope is not some weak, airy-fairy kind of thing. It takes strength to put your trust in God when life batters your heart and soul. Weaklings rarely hold on to positive expectation for long because it takes too much from them. But the spiritually strong put their trust in God and let Him lift up their hearts in hope. Then battering may come, but it cannot destroy them. Hope makes Christians stronger still.

Day 241
UNFAILING LOVE

The LORD delights in those who. . .
put their hope in his unfailing love.
PSALM 147:11

We can hope in a lot of things that fail us miserably, or we can enjoy a blind optimism that leads us into trouble. But when we hope in God, who has loved us completely, our faith cannot fail. Could the One who delights in our trust forget to bless our anticipation of an eternity with Him? Make God joyful today as you put your trust in His everlasting love.

Day 242
PROSPERITY RETURNS

*"Then I will compensate you for the
years that the swarming locust has eaten."*
JOEL 2:25 NASB

Those of us who rejoice in God can trust that
even though the consuming locusts of life destroy our blessings, God will replace them.
Though hardship makes us struggle awhile,
God turns the situation around and pours out
blessings on His faithful people. Prosperity
returns to those who love Him well, if we de-
terminedly love Him. In heaven or on earth,
the blessing appears again.

Day 243
WHERE IS YOUR HOPE?

Yes, my soul, find rest in God;
my hope comes from him.
PSALM 62:5

Those who hope in worldly things are destined for frustration and disappointment; but Christians rest in God, so instead of frustration, they receive blessing and confidence from their powerful Savior. Where is your hope today? If it's in things, you are bound to worry, but hope in God is always fulfilled. Relax in the knowledge that He never fails.

Day 244
OBEDIENCE = JOY

*"I have told you this so that my joy may be
in you and that your joy may be complete."*
JOHN 15:11

What wouldn't we do to share Jesus' complete
joy! But this verse comes after one of Jesus'
commands to obedience. Ah, now do we
change our minds? Does joy suddenly become
impossible? When Jesus calls us to act, do
we follow, or do we decide it's too hard and
give up immediately? Let's keep our eyes on
the outcome—the joy of our Lord filling our
lives. Then obedience too may become a joy.

Day 245
JOY WILL COME

My lips will shout for joy when I sing praise to you—I whom you have delivered.

PSALM 71:23

Having trouble finding joy in your life today? Do what the psalmists often did: remind yourself what God has already done for you. How many ways has following Him blessed you? Begin by thanking Him for His saving grace, and the joy starts, no matter what you face today. Your lips will show the delight in your heart.

Day 246
SORROW TO JOY

"I will turn their mourning
into gladness; I will give them
comfort and joy instead of sorrow."
JEREMIAH 31:13

In the midst of Israel's sorrow at its captivity by a pagan people, God promised a time of joy, when they would return to their land and be His people again. Are you separated from joy right now? Perhaps sin has overtaken your life, and you long to again lean close to God and share His tender love. Ask Him to turn your heart away from this barren landscape and return it to Him. Your sorrow can turn to joy.

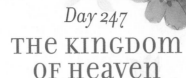

Day 247
THE KINGDOM OF HEAVEN

Sorrowful, yet always rejoicing;
poor, yet making many rich; having
nothing, and yet possessing everything.

2 CORINTHIANS 6:10

What a description of a Christian! Rejoicing in sorrow seems rather contradictory, doesn't it? How could the apostle Paul feel joy in such circumstances? Because God works in even less-than-perfect situations. In fact, He often works most powerfully when troubles load our plate. What do we have to rejoice in? The wonderful work God does in our lives, no matter what we face. We always possess the kingdom of heaven.

Day 248
PRAISE GOD—
NO MATTER WHAT

The king will rejoice in God;
all who swear by God will glory in him.
PSALM 63:11

Need some joy in your life? Start praising God, and no matter what messy situations you face today, you'll begin rejoicing. Praise Him for who He is—His immense, loving nature that has blessed you so much. Thank Him for the love He's showered on you. As you remember His love, sorrow loses its grasp on your life.

Day 249
CLOSE TO JESUS

"Be still, and know that I am God."
PSALM 46:10

So often we seek to do things for God or to prove our Christian witness. But if we become simply caught up in busyness, we lose the distinction of our faith: a close relationship with Jesus. Knowing God is not about what we do but whom we love. Our good works mean little if we disconnect from Him. Spend time being still with God today, and a deepened knowledge of Him will be your blessing.

Day 250
GOD IS GREAT

I know that the LORD is great,
that our Lord is greater than all gods.
PSALM 135:5

Other "gods" contend with Jesus in the marketplace of ideas, and devout Christians may encounter contention. But just as the psalmist recognized God's greatness, we can too as we look at the world around us. No other would-be deity shows forth its glory in creation. No other has provided His gracious salvation. If our Lord controls our lives, how can we look to any other gods?

Day 251

KNOW HIM INTIMATELY

"I will take you as my own people, and I will be your God. Then you will know that I am the LORD your God, who brought you out from under the yoke of the Egyptians."

EXODUS 6:7

God freed the Hebrews from slavery and brought them to their new land. But He didn't stop there. Today, He still proves Himself to people by freeing them from sin's slavery and creating loving relationships with them. Has God freed you from sin? Then know Him intimately. Draw near and enjoy His blessings, no matter what "slavery" you've faced before.

Day 252
FATHER AND SON

We know also that the Son of God has come
and has given us understanding, so that we
may know him who is true. And we are in him
who is true by being in his Son Jesus Christ.
He is the true God and eternal life.

1 JOHN 5:20

How do we know God? Through His Son, Jesus,
who helps us understand the love of His Father.
There is no space, no difference of opinion,
between Father and Son. When we know the
Son, we know God truly. Trust in one is trust
in both.

Day 253
LIVE DEVOTEDLY

*Do you not know that you are the temple of God
and that the Spirit of God dwells in you?*

1 CORINTHIANS 3:16 NKJV

God lives within you, not in a distant place. When you act according to His Word, He acts. When you fail, people may begin to doubt Him. That's why Paul encourages you to live devotedly for your Lord. As one of His people, you're filled with His potent Spirit, who empowers you to live a holy life. Live in His strength always.

Day 254
PERFECTING OUR LOVE

Jesus replied: " 'Love the Lord your God with all your heart and with all your soul and with all your mind.' "

MATTHEW 22:37

This simple command can be a real challenge, can't it? No matter how we try, in our own power, to love God completely, we always seem to fail somewhere. Only as God's Spirit works in our hearts will our whole being become ever more faithful. God works in us day by day, perfecting our love. Ask Him to help you love Him today.

Day 255
LOVE IS ACTION

Dear friends, let us love one another, for love comes from God. Everyone who loves has been born of God and knows God.

1 JOHN 4:7

Want to see love? Look at God. Seeking love in this world is bound to be confusing. But in our Lord, we see the clean, clear lines of real love—love we can share with our families, friends, and fellow believers. Love for our enemies. Love for our Savior. Apart from God, we cannot truly and sacrificially love others. Love isn't just a feeling; it's the actions we take as we follow Him.

Day 256
SEEING GOD

*No one has seen God at any time. If we love
one another, God abides in us, and His
love has been perfected in us.*

1 JOHN 4:12 NKJV

How do we see God? Often, it's through other
people. That's why it's important to have a
compassionate Christian witness—people see
you and think God is like you, if you claim
His name. In that way, many people have
gotten erroneous concepts about the Savior.
But many more have come to love Him through
faithful testimonies. Today, you can love others
and show them clearly what Jesus looks like.

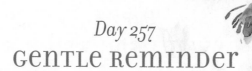

Day 257
GENTLE REMINDER

*If a man say, I love God, and hateth
his brother, he is a liar: for he that loveth
not his brother whom he hath seen, how
can he love God whom he hath not seen?*

1 JOHN 4:20 KJV

John's letter surely knows how to challenge us. Now we wonder, *Do I love God at all?* Surely, on our own, we couldn't. But when we accept God and receive His love, our attitude changes. In Jesus, we can love even a bothersome brother. Sometimes, we just need a gentle reminder.

Day 258
SWEET SACRIFICE

*Walk in the way of love, just as Christ
loved us and gave himself up for us as a
fragrant offering and sacrifice to God.*

EPHESIANS 5:2

We don't think of sacrifice as being sweet.
More often, we see it as hardship or drudgery.
But when we have experienced the delightful-
ness of Jesus' sacrifice, which brought us
into a love relationship with Him, we understand just what this verse means. Yet, God
calls us not only to receive love but to pass it
on to others who also need to understand the
sweetness of His sacrifice.

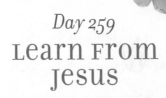

Day 259
Learn from Jesus

*"A new command I give you:
Love one another. As I have loved you,
so you must love one another."*

JOHN 13:34

How do we know how to love? We learn from Jesus. The Master had been with His disciples for three years when He spoke these words, and they had seen His love in action. We see it too in God's Word and in the lives of faithful believers. In His power, we can take what we know and follow Jesus, living out the words He spoke and the good examples we have seen.

Day 260
Take a Break

*"Only in returning to me and
resting in me will you be saved."*
ISAIAH 30:15 NLT

Some days you try everything you can think
of to save yourself, but no matter how hard
you try, you fail again and again. You fall on
your face and embarrass yourself. You hurt the
people around you. You make mistakes, and
nothing whatsoever seems to go right.

When that happens, it's time to take a
break. You need to stop trying so hard. Throw
yourself in God's arms. Rest on His grace,
knowing that He will save you.

Day 261
QUIET, GENTLE GRACE

*"Let me teach you, because I
am humble and gentle at heart,
and you will find rest for your souls."*

MATTHEW 11:29 NLT

Sometimes we keep trying to do things on our
own, even though we don't know what we're
doing and even though we're exhausted. And
all the while, Jesus waits quietly, ready to show
us the way. He will lead us with quiet, gentle
grace, carrying our burdens for us. We don't
have to try so hard. We can finally rest.

Day 262
SLEEP IN PEACE

At day's end I'm ready for sound sleep,
For you, GOD, have put my life back together.
PSALM 4:8 MSG

At the end of the day, let everything—good and bad together—drop into God's hands. You can sleep in peace, knowing that God will continue to work, healing all that is broken in your life. Relax in His grace.

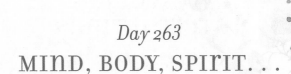

Day 263
MIND, BODY, SPIRIT...

I stretch myself out. I sleep. Then I'm
up again—rested, tall and steady.
PSALM 3:5 MSG

Rest is one of God's gifts to us, a gift we reg-
ularly need. In sleep, we are renewed, mind,
body, and spirit. Don't turn away from this
most natural and practical of gifts!

Day 264
WELCOME
INTERRUPTIONS

So they left by boat for a quiet place,
where they could be alone.
MARK 6:32 NLT

Jesus and the disciples sought a quiet place,
away from the crowds. Like us, they needed
alone time. But as so often happens, people in-
terrupt those moments of solitude. The crowd
follows us, the phone rings, someone comes
to the door. When that happens, we must ask
Jesus for the grace to follow His example and
let go of our quiet moments alone, welcoming
the interruption with patience and love.

Day 265
ALWAYS PRESENT

*LORD, you have been watching. Do not
keep quiet. Lord, do not leave me alone.*
PSALM 35:22 NCV

Have you ever seen a child suddenly look up
from playing, realize she's all alone, and then
run to get her mother's attention? Meanwhile,
her mother was watching her all along. Sometimes solitude is a good thing—and other times,
it's just plain lonely. When loneliness turns
into isolation, remember that God's loving
eyes are always on you. He will never leave
you all alone, and His grace is always present.

Day 266
ALL ALONE

"But when you pray, go away by yourself,
shut the door behind you, and pray to your
Father in private. Then your Father, who
sees everything, will reward you."

MATTHEW 6:6 NLT

Prayer takes many shapes and forms. There's
the corporate kind of prayer, in which we stand
in a pew in a church, lifting our hearts to God
as part of a congregation. There is also the far
less elaborate kind of prayer that is said quickly
and on the run; the whispered cry for help or
song of praise in the midst of life's busyness.
But we need to make at least some time in our
lives for the prayer that comes out of solitude,
when, in the privacy of some quiet place, we
meet God's grace all alone.

Day 267
THE RIGHT PEOPLE

*The Lord God said, "It isn't good
for the man to live alone. I need
to make a suitable partner for him."*
GENESIS 2:18 CEV

God understands that human beings need each
other. His love comes to us through others.
That is the way He designed us, and we can
trust His grace to bring the right people along
when we need them, the people who will
banish our loneliness and share our lives.

Day 268

praise him!

The Lord is my strength, my song,
and my salvation. He is my God,
and I will praise him.

EXODUS 15:2 TLB

God makes you strong; He makes you sing with gladness; and He rescues you from sin. These are the gifts of His grace. When He has given you so much, don't you want to give back to Him? Use your strength, your joy, and your freedom to praise Him.

Day 269
TODAY—AND TOMORROW

*You are my strong shield, and I trust you
completely. You have helped me, and I
will celebrate and thank you in song.*
PSALM 28:7 CEV

God proves Himself to us over and over again.
And yet over and over, we doubt His power.
We need to learn from experience. The God
whose strength rescued us yesterday and
the day before will certainly rescue us again
today. As we celebrate the grace we received
yesterday and the day before, we gain confidence and faith for today and tomorrow.

Day 270
LIFTED UP

*But those who trust in the LORD will find new
strength. They will soar high on wings like
eagles. They will run and not grow weary.
They will walk and not faint.*

ISAIAH 40:31 NLT

Do you ever have days when you ask yourself,
"How much further can I go? How much longer can I keep going like this?" On days like
that, you long to give up. You wish you could
just run away from the world and hide. Trust
God's grace to give you the strength you need,
even then. Let Him lift you up on eagles' wings.

Day 271
WHERE CREDIT IS DUE

It is not that we think we are
qualified to do anything on our own.
Our qualification comes from God.
2 Corinthians 3:5 NLT

It's easy to seek God when we feel like failures, but when success comes our way, we like to congratulate ourselves rather than give God the credit. When we achieve great things, we need to remember that it is God's grace through us that brought about our success.

Day 272
careful plans

*Without good advice everything
goes wrong—it takes careful
planning for things to go right.*
PROVERBS 15:22 CEV

The Bible reminds us that when we start a new
venture, we should not trust success to come
automatically. We need to seek the advice of
those we trust. We need to make careful plans.
And most of all, we need to seek God's counsel, praying for the grace and wisdom to do
things right.

Day 273
wonderful!

Commit your actions to the LORD,
and your plans will succeed.
PROVERBS 16:3 NLT

Just because we *want* something to happen, doesn't mean it will, no matter how hard we pray. We've all found that out (often to our sorrow!). But when we truly commit everything we do to God, praying only for His grace to be given free rein in our lives, then we will be surprised by what comes about. It may not be what we imagined—but it will be wonderful!

Day 274
whatever comes next

*"You will succeed in whatever you choose to do,
and light will shine on the road ahead of you."*
JOB 22:28 NLT

The word *success* originally meant simply "the thing that comes next." Over the years, we've added to that meaning the sense that success has to be the thing we wanted to happen, the outcome for which we hoped. But God does not necessarily define success the way we do. Whatever comes next, no matter what, His grace transforms it, using circumstances to create the light we need to travel still farther on our road to heaven.

Day 275
VEHICLE FOR
GOD'S GRACE

*Do not neglect your gift. . . . Be diligent in
these matters; give yourself wholly to them,
so that everyone may see your progress.*
1 TIMOTHY 4:14–15

God expects us to use the talents He gave us.
Don't turn away from them with a false sense
of modesty. Exercise them. Improve your
skills. Whatever your gift may be, use it as a
vehicle for God's grace.

Day 276

From God

*There are different kinds of gifts,
but they are all from the same Spirit.*

1 Corinthians 12:4 NCV

God shines through us in different ways.
One person is good at expressing herself in
words; another is good with children; and still
another has a gift for giving wise counsel to her
friends. Whatever our gifts are, they all come
from God. They are all tangible expressions
of His grace.

Day 277
USE YOUR GIFT

Each of you has been blessed with one
of God's many wonderful gifts to be used
in the service of others. So use your gift well.
1 PETER 4:10 CEV

God did not give you your talents for your
own pleasure only. These skills you have were
meant to be offered to the world. He wants to
use them to build His kingdom here on earth.
So, pick up your skill, whatever it is, and use
it to bring grace to someone's life.

Day 278
creative expression

Not only has the Lord filled him with his Spirit, but he has given him wisdom and made him a skilled craftsman who can create objects of art.
EXODUS 35:31 CEV

We were designed to be creative people. Whether we sew clothes or paint pictures, come up with new business ideas or write stories, make a welcoming home or cook delicious meals, God's creativity longs to be expressed through us. As we exercise our creative talents, we are united with Him. His Spirit works through our hands, creating visions of grace as we make the world a lovelier place for us all.

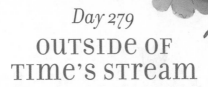

Day 279
OUTSIDE OF TIME'S STREAM

Your throne, O Lord, has stood from time immemorial. You yourself are from the everlasting past.
PSALM 93:2 NLT

If you think of time as a fast-moving river, then we are creatures caught in its stream, thrust ever forward into the future, while the past rushes away behind us. Life keeps slipping away from us like water between our fingers. But God is outside of time's stream. He holds our past safely in His hands, and His grace is permanent and unshakable. His love is the lifesaver to which we cling in the midst of time's wild waves.

Day 280

MEANT TO MOVE

*We are only foreigners living here on
earth for a while, just as our ancestors
were. And we will soon be gone, like a
shadow that suddenly disappears.*

1 CHRONICLES 29:15 CEV

We are not meant to feel too at home in this
world. Maybe that is why time is designed to
keep us from lingering too long in one place.
We are meant to be moving on, making our
way to our forever-home in heaven. Grace
has brought us safe thus far—and grace will
lead us home.

Day 281

YOUNG

Honor and enjoy your Creator
while you're still young.
ECCLESIASTES 12:1 MSG

Young is a matter of perspective. Some people are old at fifteen, and others are still young at ninety. As we enjoy the God who made us, honoring Him in all we do, His grace will keep us young.

Day 282
SENSE OF TIMING

But do not forget this one thing, dear friends:
With the Lord a day is like a thousand years,
and a thousand years are like a day.

2 PETER 3:8

God's sense of timing is not the same as ours. What seems like forever to us, an impossible time to wait for something, God sees as exactly the right amount of time, a mere blink of the eye. On the other hand, God's grace can use a split second to change a person's life.

Day 283
LOOKS CAN BE DECEIVING

Therefore we do not lose heart.
Though outwardly we are wasting away,
yet inwardly we are being renewed day by day.
2 CORINTHIANS 4:16

On the outside, people see us getting older and frailer, but looks are deceiving. As Christians, we constantly build our belief if we walk consistently with God. We're growing deeper in faith, being spiritually renewed every day. God's glory lies ahead of us, as on earth we learn to appreciate His love and compassion. Undaunted, we look ahead to eternity and a new body, made perfect by our Savior.

Day 284
LIFE-ALTERING IMPACT

We were therefore buried with him through baptism into death in order that, just as Christ was raised from the dead through the glory of the Father, we too may live a new life.

ROMANS 6:4

Baptism is a picture of the old, sinful nature's death and the new faith-life God gives those who trust in Him. Belief in Jesus has a life-altering impact. One moment, a sinful person is dead, held in sin's grasp. The next, she becomes an entirely new person, alive in her Savior. Only Jesus offers this glorious freedom. Has He given it to you?

Day 285
LIVING IN THE LIGHT

In him was life, and that life
was the light of all mankind.
JOHN 1:4

Jesus is a Christian's life and light, as anyone
who has walked with Him for a while can tell
you. Everything is different once He enters a
soul. As a result, the new believer begins to
make changes, cleaning out the dark corners
of her existence so that the bright light shining within her will not fall on dirty places.
She's living in the light, following Jesus.

Day 286
NEW LIFE

Therefore, if anyone is in Christ, he is a new creation; old things have passed away; behold, all things have become new.

2 CORINTHIANS 5:17 NKJV

New life in Christ: what indescribable freedom to be separated from our sin! No longer bound by it but able to live in Him, we joyfully race into our new existence.

But in time, our tendency to fall into sin tarnishes God's gift. Suddenly, we don't feel so new. "Old" Christians need only turn again to Christ for forgiveness, and the Spirit's cleansing makes us new again.

Day 287
CELEBRATE YOUR NEWNESS

If Christ is in you, the body is dead
because of sin, but the Spirit is
life because of righteousness.
ROMANS 8:10 NKJV

Know Jesus? Then your body and your fleshly
desires are less important than your spirit.
Because Jesus lives in you, sin has no permanent claim on your life. Though it tempts
you and you may give in for a time, it no longer has a firm grasp on all your days. You can
turn aside from it and dwell in your Lord instead. Celebrate your newness in Jesus: live for
Him today!

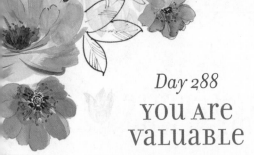

Day 288
YOU ARE VALUABLE

Who can find a virtuous woman?
for her price is far above rubies.
PROVERBS 31:10 KJV

Are you a virtuous woman? If so, you are truly valuable, no matter how unbelievers criticize you. Proverbs 31 says you can have a profitable life with good relationships, a happy home life, and successful business ventures if you run your life according to God's principles. So, don't worry about the opinions of others if they don't mesh with God's. Instead, obey Him and be a valuable jewel to your Lord.

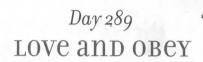

Day 289
LOVE AND OBEY

*"Whoever has my commands and
keeps them is the one who loves me."*
JOHN 14:21

Do you feel you love God with all your heart?
Then show it by obeying Him. Jesus paved
the path for you. Through His own sacrificial
life, He showed you what it means to obey the
Father. A Christian who lives for herself rather
than for God shows wavering commitment.
One who loves God wholeheartedly walks in
Jesus' way, obeying His commands in scripture. Here is where we start: Love God? Then
obey Him too.

Day 290
BLESSINGS WILL COME

"All these blessings shall come upon you and overtake you, because you obey the voice of the Lord your God."
DEUTERONOMY 28:2 NKJV

Obey God; receive blessings. It seems simple enough, doesn't it? Then why do we obey and only get in more trouble than before? Perhaps it's because we're looking at it from our perspective, not His. Blessings do not always follow on the heels of obedience; they often take time to appear. Today's blessings may result from long-ago faithfulness. But because God has promised, we know good things come, if only we wait.

Day 291
INTO ETERNITY

Blessed are they that do his commandments,
that they may have right to the tree of life,
and may enter in through the gates into the city.
REVELATION 22:14 KJV

The blessings of obedience not only impact us
today; they follow us into eternity. Whatever
we do to please God never dies. By trusting
in Jesus, the works that demonstrate our faith
give us joy now and remain secure for the
future in the One who never changes. We look
forward to life in the New Jerusalem even as
we reap His blessings now.

Day 292
Prayer—Give and Receive

Brothers and sisters, pray for us.
1 Thessalonians 5:25

Do you find it hard to ask others to pray for you? Don't be afraid to take that step into humility. Paul wasn't, when he asked the Thessalonians to pray for his ministry. Being part of the church requires an interdependence of prayers given and received. As a congregation prays for each other, their spirits connect in a new, caring way. Carefully choose those with whom you share private concerns, but never fear to ask a mature Christian to pray for you.

Day 293
THE BEST ANSWER

Pray without ceasing.
1 THESSALONIANS 5:17 KJV

Haven't received an answer to your prayer? Don't give up. There's no time limit on speaking to God about your needs. It's just that we often work on a different time schedule from God. We want an answer yesterday, while He has something better in mind for tomorrow. So, keep praying. God listens to His children and gives them the best answer, not the fastest one.

Day 294
GOD HEARS

"Therefore I tell you, whatever you ask for in prayer, believe that you have received it, and it will be yours."

MARK 11:24

This verse is not prescribing some magical incantation, but faith that God hears and answers our requests. When we trust that He knows our needs and wants to respond to them, we are in a position to receive. Would Jesus be proud of our requests? Do we seek the good of others? Or do we look only to our own desires? God answers prayers that reflect His will. How do yours stack up against this measure?

Day 295
TURN TO HIM

Rejoicing in hope, patient in tribulation,
continuing steadfastly in prayer.
ROMANS 12:12 NKJV

When do you pray the most, in times of ease
or trial? Like most folks, you probably bend
God's ear when you're hurting physically or
spiritually, and that makes sense. For who
helps the way God does? Paul describes the
Christian's best response to trouble in these
pithy phrases. While the faithless might rail
against God, complaining that He is unfair,
Christians know otherwise. We have a hope,
a reason for patience, and a Father who cares.
Let's turn to Him no matter what our need.

Day 296

LOVE YOUR ENEMY

*"But I tell you, love your enemies
and pray for those who persecute you."*
MATTHEW 5:44

Without God's strength, could any of us follow this command of Jesus for more than a very brief time? Consistently loving an enemy is a real challenge. If you hurt from pain inflicted by another, you hardly want to pray for her. But loving actions and prayer can bring great peace between two people at odds with each other. For those who consistently follow this command, strife may not last forever.

Day 297
HEALING POWER

The prayer of faith will save the sick,
and the Lord will raise him up. And if
he has committed sins, he will be forgiven.

JAMES 5:15 NKJV

Have you seen the amazing healing power of prayer? As faithful Christians lift a sufferer up to God, He works in the body, but also in the heart and soul. Know someone who is ill? Pray for physical health to return. But don't forget to include spiritual needs, for the Great Physician treats the whole person. Some spiritual issue may be the real problem that requires healing.

Day 298
PRAYER FROM THE HEART

Some trust in chariots, and some in horses; but we will remember the name of the LORD our God.

PSALM 20:7 NKJV

This may seem an odd prayer for a king going out to battle, but it shows where David's heart was. He knew his war equipment could fail, but God could not. What danger can we face that God is incapable of defending us from? None. Where have we placed our trust—in Him or in worldly defenses?

Day 299
overcoming
the sin barrier

*Godly sorrow brings repentance that
leads to salvation and leaves no regret.*

2 CORINTHIANS 7:10

Godly sorrow comes when we feel the pain of
our own sins. As we recognize our own wrong-
doing and know that our actions have hurt us,
others, and even the heart of God, we reach the
place to do something about it. We repent, and
God offers His salvation.

Has sin come between you and your Savior? Turn at once in sorrow, and ask Him to
make everything right in your heart and soul.
You'll never be sorry you did.

Day 300
CLEANSING SPIRIT

I came not to call the righteous,
but sinners to repentance.
LUKE 5:32 KJV

Repentance isn't meant for "good people" who only have "tiny" sins to confess. This verse reminds us that no sin is too awful for God to hear about it. God calls all who are sinful—those who most need Him and have the most to fear from His awesome holiness. Each of us may hesitate to confess sins and admit to wrongs that embarrass us. But we are just the ones He calls. One moment of repentance, and His Spirit cleanses our lives.

Day 301
BLESSING BEHIND REPENTANCE

"Repent, then, and turn to God, so that your sins may be wiped out, that times of refreshing may come from the Lord."
ACTS 3:19

When we consider repentance, we tend to think it's hard. That's only because we're shortsighted. Giving up sin may not appeal to our hardened hearts because we're not looking at the blessing set behind repentance. Yet as we turn from sin, we feel the refreshing breath of God's Spirit bringing new life to our lives. Then, does anything seem difficult?

Day 302
COMPASSION TO OTHERS

"And if he sins against you seven times in a day, and seven times in a day returns to you, saying, 'I repent,' you shall forgive him."
LUKE 17:4 NKJV

When another offends us, do we pass on the forgiveness we have received? That's what Jesus commanded. Remembering how gracious God has been to us, we need to show it to those who affront us too. As we think of our many sins that God put behind His back, can we fail to show compassion to others?

Day 303

AVAILABLE 24-7

*"Blessed is the man to whom
the LORD shall not impute sin."*

ROMANS 4:8 NKJV

Sin forgiven: what a wonderful thought! No longer do we need to be dragged into wrong-doing, because God has cleansed our hearts. His Spirit sweeps through us, lifting the burden of sin from our lives. Though we still fail, in Christ, God will not hold the sin against us. Forgiveness, available 24-7, sends His Spirit through our lives again and again.

Day 304
ADORNED
WITH GRACE

Don't ever forget kindness and truth.
Wear them like a necklace.
PROVERBS 3:3 NCV

Kindness and truth are strands of the same necklace. You should not be so kind that you evade the truth, nor should you be so truthful that you wound others. Instead, adorn yourselves with both strands of this necklace. Wear it with grace.

Day 305
WHAT'S REAL

*"Then you will experience for yourselves
the truth, and the truth will free you."*
JOHN 8:32 MSG

Truth is what is real, while lies are nothing
but words. God wants us to experience what
is truly real. Sometimes we would rather hide
from reality, but grace comes to us through
truth. No matter how painful the truth may
sometimes seem, it will ultimately set us free.

Day 306
ON TRUTH'S SIDE

We're rooting for the truth to win out in you.
We couldn't possibly do otherwise.
2 CORINTHIANS 13:8 MSG

As we look at the world around us, we can see
that people often prefer falsehoods to truth.
They choose to live in a world that soothes
their anxiety rather than face life's reality. We
cannot force people to acknowledge what they
don't want to face, but we can do everything
possible to encourage them and build them
up. We can cheer for the truth, trusting that
God's grace is always on truth's side.

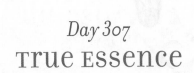

Day 307
TRUE ESSENCE

"God is spirit, and those who worship him must worship in spirit and truth."
JOHN 4:24 NCV

We might be able to fool the flesh-and-blood people around us, but we cannot deceive the Spirit of God. He sees our truest essence. The only way to come into His presence is to accept our own truth—and offer it up to Him. May He give us the grace to truly worship Him!

Day 308
THE MISSING PIECES

Trust the LORD with all your heart, and don't depend on your own understanding.
PROVERBS 3:5 NCV

Life is confusing. No matter how hard we try, we can't always make sense of it. We don't like it when that happens, and so we keep trying to determine what's going on, as though we were trying puzzle piece after puzzle piece to fill in a picture we long to see. Sometimes, though, we have to accept that in this life we will never be able to see the entire image. We have to trust God's grace for the missing pieces.

Day 309
GROWING IN GRACE

*This is my prayer for you: that your love
will grow more and more; that you will have
knowledge and understanding with your love.*

PHILIPPIANS 1:9 NCV

God wants us to be spiritually mature. He wants
us to love more deeply, and at the same time,
He wants us to reach deeper into wisdom and
understanding. This is not something we can
accomplish in our own strength with our own
abilities. Only God can make us grow in grace.

Day 310
MOST IMPORTANT

Tune your ears to the world of Wisdom;
set your heart on a life of Understanding.
PROVERBS 2:3 MSG

What do you listen to most? Do you hear the
world's voice telling you to buy, buy, buy; to
dress and look a certain way; to focus on things
that won't last? Or have you tuned your ears
to hear the quiet voice of God's wisdom? You
can tell the answer to that question by your
response to yet another question: What is most
important to you? Things? Or the intangible
grace of true understanding?

Day 311
WALKING WITH GRACE

*"Give me an understanding heart so that
I can govern your people well and know
the difference between right and wrong."*
1 KINGS 3:9 NLT

We are not kings who rule nations, but all of
us have spheres of influence and authority,
whether at home or at work. As Christ's followers, we must be careful not to abuse our
authority. Instead, we should seek to understand, to walk with grace the straight path of
kindness and wisdom.

Day 312
FIRST PRIORITIES

*For Wisdom is better than all the
trappings of wealth; nothing you
could wish for holds a candle to her.*
PROVERBS 8:11 MSG

What do you value most? You may know the
answer you are "supposed" to give to that
question, but you can tell the real answer by
where your time and energy are focused. Do
you spend most of your time working for and
thinking about money and physical wealth,
or do you make wisdom and grace your first
priorities?

Day 313
GRACE MULTIPLIED

Honor the LORD with your wealth and with
the best part of everything you produce.
PROVERBS 3:9 NLT

We connect the word *wealth* with money, but long ago the word meant "happiness, prosperity, well-being." If you think about your wealth in this light, the word encompasses far more of your life. Your health, your abilities, your friends, your family, your physical strength, and your creative energy—all these are parts of your true wealth. Grace brought all these riches into your life, and when we use them to honor God, grace is multiplied still more.

Day 314
NEVER BOUGHT

They trust in their riches and brag
about all of their wealth. You cannot
buy back your life or pay off God!
PSALM 49:6–7 CEV

We humans are easily confused about what real
wealth is. We think that money can make us
strong. We assume that physical possessions
will enhance our importance and dignity in
others' eyes. But life is not for sale, and grace
can never be bought.

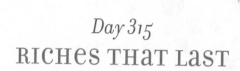

Day 315
RICHES THAT LAST

*"Yes, a person is a fool to store up
earthly wealth but not have a
rich relationship with God."*
LUKE 12:21 NLT

Why would we want money in the bank and a
house full of stuff if we lived in a world that
was empty of grace? Only in God do we find
the riches that will last forever.

Day 316
WISE ENOUGH TO LEAD

"To God belong wisdom and power;
counsel and understanding are his."
JOB 12:13

The word *wisdom* comes from the same root
words that have to do with vision, the ability to
see into a deeper spiritual reality. Where else
can we turn for the grace to see beneath life's
surface except to God? Who else can we trust
to be strong enough and wise enough to lead
us to our eternal home?

Day 317
BUILDING GOD'S KINGDOM

*And I have filled him with the Spirit of God,
in wisdom and ability, in understanding
and intelligence, and in knowledge,
and in all kinds of craftsmanship.*
EXODUS 31:3 AMPC

Your abilities, your intelligence, your knowledge, and your talents are all gifts of grace from God's generous Spirit. But without wisdom, the ability to see into the spiritual world, none of these gifts is worth very much. Wisdom is what makes all the other pieces fit together, allowing us to use our talents to build God's spiritual kingdom.

Day 318
NOTHING MORE VALUABLE

*Wisdom is more valuable than gold
and crystal. It cannot be purchased
with jewels mounted in fine gold.*

JOB 28:17 NLT

Money can't buy you love—and it can't buy
wisdom either. Wisdom is more precious than
anything this world has to offer. In fact, some
passages of the Old Testament seem to indicate
that Wisdom is another name for Jesus. Just
as Jesus is the Way, the Truth, and the Light,
He is also the One who gives us the vision to
see God's world all around us. No other gift is
more valuable than Jesus.

Day 319
secret places

Yet, you desire truth and sincerity.
Deep down inside me you teach me wisdom.
PSALM 51:6 GW

Sometimes we are like Adam and Eve in the garden after they had sinned; we are afraid to come naked into God's presence. We think we can hide ourselves from Him. But God cannot teach our hearts if we refuse to be open with Him. We must take the risk of stepping into His presence with complete honesty and vulnerability. When we do, His grace touches us at our deepest, most secret places, and we are filled with His wisdom.

Day 320
CONTROL

Put GOD in charge of your work,
then what you've planned will take place.
PROVERBS 16:3 MSG

If we're doing a job that is important to us,
it is hard to let go of our control. Not only do
we hate to trust someone else to take over,
but we often don't want to trust God to take
charge either. We want to do it all by ourselves.
But the best laid plans fall into nothing without God's help. What's more, as we rely on His
grace, we no longer need to feel stressed or
pressured! We can let Him take charge.

Day 321
HEAVEN'S PERSPECTIVE

*Always give yourselves fully to the work
of the Lord, because you know that
your labor in the Lord is not in vain.*

1 CORINTHIANS 15:58

Sometimes you may feel as though all your hard work comes to nothing. But if your work is the Lord's work, you can trust Him to bring it to fulfillment. You may not always know what is being accomplished in the light of eternity, but God knows. And when you look back from heaven's perspective, you will be able to see how much grace was accomplished through all your hard work.

Day 322
THE BIGGER PICTURE

"But you, be strong and do not lose courage,
for there is reward for your work."
2 CHRONICLES 15:7 NASB

Why do you work? For a paycheck? For respect? For a sense of self-worth? All are good
reasons to work, but never forget that your
work is part of a bigger picture. God wants to
use your hands, your intelligence, and your
efforts to build His kingdom, the place where
grace dwells.

Day 323
RECONCILERS

God was reconciling the world to himself
in Christ, not counting people's sins
against them. And he has committed
to us the message of reconciliation.

2 CORINTHIANS 5:19

The Lord loved you so much that He paid a
huge price to draw you into His arms. Jesus'
sacrifice destroyed the sin barrier that sep-
arates humanity and God. Those who repent
are reconciled to their holy God, but faith
does not stop there. He makes us reconcil-
ers as He sends us out with the message that
has meant so much: "God loves you too."

Day 324
saving grace

Truly my soul finds rest in God;
my salvation comes from him.
PSALM 62:1

At the moment you repented of your sins and asked Jesus to control your life, God saved you. But He didn't stop there. Each day of your life, He continues His saving work. He redirects you, protects you, and provides for your every need. In any trouble, rest in Him. He will not fail.

Day 325
SHINE FOR HIM

[Jesus] gave himself for us to redeem us from all
wickedness and to purify for himself a people
that are his very own, eager to do what is good.

TITUS 2:14

Is there any sin from which Jesus cannot
save us? No. As long as we look to Him, He
will lead us into increasing, joyous holiness. God takes sinful people and changes
their lives, making them His hands in an
evil world. As His people draw near to Him,
putting off sin, their good works shine
forth the nature of their Savior. Will you
shine for Him today?

Day 326
our partner

*Continue to work out your
salvation with fear and trembling.*
PHILIPPIANS 2:12

Salvation is hard work! Not only did it require Jesus' crucifixion for our sins, but we have a part in the effort too. We have to live out the commands in God's Word that make our faith impact our world. But we need not feel discouraged, for we are not alone in the labor. God acts through us by His Spirit. What better working partner could we have than God Himself?

Day 327
THE GLORY OF JESUS

God chose you as firstfruits to be saved. . . .
He called you. . .that you might share
in the glory of our Lord Jesus Christ.
2 THESSALONIANS 2:13–14

Did you know you share Jesus' glory? Not
because you are doing a wonderful job as a
Christian, but simply because He decided
to call you to Himself. God chose to share
Himself with you and make you like His Son.
Daily, He calls you to learn more of His
magnificence as you faithfully follow Him.
Isn't it wonderful to share just a bit of God's
greatness?

Day 328

SPIRITUAL TRAINING

All Scripture. . .is useful for. . .
training in righteousness, so that
the servant of God may be thoroughly
equipped for every good work.
2 TIMOTHY 3:16–17

Did you realize that God prepares you to do good works every day of your life? Because you believe in Him, He will lead you to do good, following His plan for your life.

How do you start? By reading the scriptures, His guidebook. There you will learn what to believe, how to act, and how to speak with love. Soon you'll be ready to put into action all you've learned.

serving others

*You. . .were called to be free. But do not
use your freedom to indulge the flesh;
rather, serve one another humbly in love.*

GALATIANS 5:13

As women, we know a lot about serving. We
serve on many fronts and sometimes wonder why this is our lot. God tells us He freed
us from sin, not to do what we like but so we
can share His love. If we're tempted to fulfill
our own sinful desires, let's remind ourselves
why we are here—we obey Jesus by doing
good for others. If that's not our goal, we need
redirection from Him.

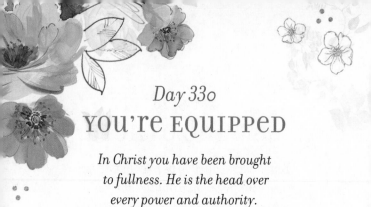

Day 330
YOU'RE EQUIPPED

*In Christ you have been brought
to fullness. He is the head over
every power and authority.*
COLOSSIANS 2:10

Do you feel incomplete or inadequate, unable
to carry out the tasks God has given you? You
aren't, you know, if you tap into His Spirit. God
equips you to do all things in Him. If you feel
overwhelmed, make sure you haven't taken
on tasks rightfully belonging to someone else.
God does not overload your life with busyness.
He has a purpose for all you do. So be certain
you're serving in the right place, doing the
work He planned for you.

Day 331
MAKE THE MOST

Since everything will be destroyed in this way,
what kind of people ought you to be?
You ought to live holy and godly lives.
2 PETER 3:11

Knowing that the world will not last forever,
how should we act? We have no devil-may-care
option, in which we act as if eternity did not
matter, because God calls us to live wholly
for Him. The world's destruction should not
make us careless, but vigilant to make the
most of our time. In the end, all we do here
will not be lost but will pass into eternity.

Day 332
YOU HAVE GIFTS!

Now to each one the manifestation of
the Spirit is given for the common good.

1 CORINTHIANS 12:7

Did you know that you are a gifted person? God gives each of His children spiritual gifts designed to help themselves and others— wisdom, knowledge, faith, healing, to name just a few. As you grow spiritually, you begin to unwrap those presents from God. Over time, you may be surprised and blessed at how many He's provided for you. Feeling unimportant? Remind yourself that you're gifted by God!

Day 333
GRACE IS A GIFT

But unto every one of us is given grace
according to the measure of the gift of Christ.
EPHESIANS 4:7 KJV

We don't usually think of grace as a "spiritual gift." But consider: it's the basis for all the gifts God gives us. Without His gracious forgiveness, we'd have nothing spiritually. Our sins so separate us that only His forgiveness allows us to approach Him. Whether we receive a large measure of grace or a smaller one, it is the perfect gift, given by Jesus, just for us. Let's appreciate what it cost Him and walk in Him today.

Day 334
FOR HIS GLORY

*We have different gifts, according
to the grace given to each of us.*

ROMANS 12:6

Your spiritual gifts are tailored especially
for you. God has a purpose for your life. To
help you accomplish it, He has given just the
gifts you need—nothing more, nothing less.
Doesn't knowing that God has gifted you in
just the right way make you feel special? Thank
Him for those gifts today, and use them for
the glory of His kingdom and to help others.

Day 335
REACH OUT

Try to excel in those [gifts]
that build up the church.
1 CORINTHIANS 14:12

Paul's words to the Corinthians were meant
for us too. We should build up the church, not
ourselves, through our spiritual gifts. When
God gave you a special combination of spiritual abilities, it wasn't to make you feel important. He designed them to help you reach
out to those who need to accept Him as Savior
and to support believers who also have your
mission to reach the world. Is that how you're
using your gifts today?

Day 336
IN HIS POWER

I can do all things through
Christ who strengthens me.
PHILIPPIANS 4:13 NKJV

Need strength? Turn to God for all you need.
Why take on life by yourself when He offers
all you need? Often, as obedient Christians,
we make great efforts with our feeble spiritual
muscles. But ultimately, our own strength
always fails. When Christ's Spirit works
through us, the Christian life flows smoothly;
in His power we accomplish His purposes.
Today, is Christ bearing the burden or are we?
Only He has the might we need in our lives.

Day 337
CHRISTIAN STRENGTH

*Finally, be strong in the Lord
and in his mighty power.*
EPHESIANS 6:10

When you rely on God's strength, what are you tapping into? Not some small pool of power that fails at a critical moment. The Christian's strength is mighty because God is mighty. He who created the universe does not have a short arm that cannot reach down to your situation. Shining stars testify to His authority. Galaxies in space are ordered by His hand. Cannot He order your life too? Ask Him to use His strength in your life, and you will have all you need.

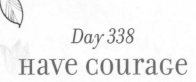

Day 338
Have Courage

Be on your guard; stand firm in
the faith; be courageous; be strong.
1 Corinthians 16:13

Being a Christian can take lots of courage. As
the world around us becomes increasingly
hostile to God and our personal lives become
tense because of our beliefs, we feel the challenge. But we are not defenseless. Christians
through the ages have faced these troubles and
triumphed. The Lord who supported them
gives us strength too. Let us stand fast for Jesus,
calling on His Spirit to strengthen our lives.
Then we will be strong indeed.

Day 339
UPLIFT OTHERS

We who are strong ought to bear
with the failings of the weak
and not to please ourselves.
ROMANS 15:1

So, God has made you strong in some area—
perhaps by experience, as you have struggled
to obey Him. Now, how do you respond to others? Don't criticize those who have different
experiences or other strengths, or carp about
the failings of new, weak Christians. Instead,
use your power to uplift others. Come alongside and help. Then God's strength will have
helped you both.

Day 340
DAILY SEEK HIS STRENGTH

Our sufficiency is from God.
2 CORINTHIANS 3:5 NKJV

Feel unable to take on life? Paul knows how you feel. He didn't see himself as the perfect apostle we often think he was. Knowing his own flaws and failures, Paul recognized the work Jesus did in him every day. God made His servant sufficient to his tasks. He'll do it for you too as you walk in faith and seek His strength.

YOU WILL PROSPER

Do not turn from [the law] to the right hand
or to the left, that you may prosper wherever
you go. This Book of the Law shall not depart
from your mouth, but you shall meditate in
it day and night, that you may observe to do
according to all that is written in it. For then
you will make your way prosperous, and
then you will have good success.

JOSHUA 1:7–8 NKJV

God promised success to Joshua if he obeyed
His Word. That promise works for you too.
But sometimes you may not feel that obeying
God has brought you great prosperity. Just
wait. It may take time, the success may not
take the form you expect, or you may not see
the results until you reach heaven, but God will
prosper those who do His will. He promised
it, and His promises never fail.

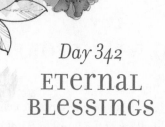

Day 342
ETERNAL BLESSINGS

*A faithful man will abound
with blessings, but he who hastens
to be rich will not go unpunished.*
PROVERBS 28:20 NKJV

Faithfulness to God or success in the world:
Have you had to choose between them? Seeking
the world's goals brings short-term benefits,
but only God provides abundant and ongoing
blessings for those who put serving Him first
in their lives. Though worldly blessings last for
a day, a year, or a few years, they cannot remain
for eternity. When you consider success, think
of the kind that really lasts.

Day 343
LIVING IN HIM

The meek will inherit the land
and enjoy peace and prosperity.
PSALM 37:11

You might call this God's definition of success: a profitable land that provides for His people and His peace that provides a blessed life. Notice that money and other possessions aren't mentioned. But the peace of living in Him flows freely to those who abide in Him. Would this be success to you? If not, what does it tell you about your spiritual life?

Day 344
real success

Save now, we beseech You,
O Lord; send now prosperity, O Lord,
we beseech You, and give to us success!
PSALM 118:25 AMPC

Is it wrong to pray for success? No. But notice that the Bible connects success to God's salvation. Prosperity or any other achievement means little when it's separated from God's will and our obedience to Him. When you ask to attain something, do you also seek God's saving grace in that part of your life? If so, you'll have real success—spiritual and temporal blessings.

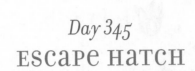

Day 345
ESCAPE HATCH

No temptation has overtaken you except what is common to mankind. And God is faithful. . . . When you are tempted, he will also provide a way out so that you can endure it.
1 CORINTHIANS 10:13

No matter how powerful it seems, you need not give in to temptation. God always provides you with an escape hatch. When temptation pulls at you, turn your eyes to Jesus. Replace that tempting object with Him, and you will not fall.

Day 346
ASK JESUS

*Because he himself suffered when
he was tempted, he is able to help
those who are being tempted.*

HEBREWS 2:18

Why can Jesus help us when temptation
strikes? Because He's walked a mile in our
shoes. He knows how strongly sin attracts
us. But because He never fell prey to it, He
can effectively show us how to resist even the
strongest enticement. The biggest mistakes
we make are not calling on Him and not per-
sistently seeking His powerful aid when Satan
repeatedly lures us into sin. Need help? Just
ask Jesus.

Day 347
Lean on Jesus

*"Therefore if the Son makes you free,
you shall be free indeed."*
JOHN 8:36 NKJV

Sometimes we don't feel freed from sin. Temptations draw us, even though we love Jesus. So, His words here can be both comforting and challenging. The Jews wanted to trust in their spiritual history, not God. That plan didn't work well for them, and it won't work for us, either. We can't rely on history or our past deeds to put sin behind us. What will work? Leaning on Jesus every day, trusting Him to make us free indeed!

Day 348
GOD IS GREATER

*Each person is tempted when they
are dragged away by their own
evil desire and enticed.*

JAMES 1:14

God does not draw us into temptation. He is
holy, unable to tempt anyone into wrongdoing.
The attraction for sin comes from within us
because our evil desires lead us toward sin.
When we face situations that encourage our
own wickedness, they are not designed by God
to make us fall. Instead, they provide opportunities to turn to Him and progressively turn
away from iniquity. No evil within us is so great
that God is not greater still.

Day 349
GOD'S PROTECTION

The Lord knows how to deliver the godly out
of temptations and to reserve the unjust under
punishment for the day of judgment.
2 PETER 2:9 NKJV

Feeling surrounded by temptations? God
hasn't forgotten you. He knows how to protect His children from harm and offers His
wisdom to His children. Maybe you need to
avoid places that could lead you into sin—that
may mean finding a new job or new friends.
When God is trying to protect you, don't resist.
Sin is never better than knowing Him.

Day 350
GIVE THANKS

Give thanks to the God of gods.
His love endures forever.
PSALM 136:2

———————————————

Having trouble being thankful? Read Psalm
136. You'll be reminded of the wonders of
God's power and His enduring love. The God
who protected Israel watches over you too.
Even when there may be little in your life to
rejoice about, you can always delight in Him.
Give thanks to God. He has not forgotten you.
His love endures forever.

Day 351
GOD SAVES

I will give you thanks, for you answered me;
you have become my salvation.

PSALM 118:21

A new believer didn't write this verse. The psalmist thanks God not just for loving him enough to tear him from the claws of original sin; instead, this mature man of faith recognizes that God saves him every day, whenever he is in trouble. God does this in your life too. What salvation has He worked in your life recently? What thanks do you need to offer Him now?

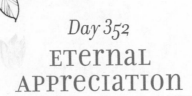

Day 352
ETERNAL APPRECIATION

LORD my God, I will praise you forever.
PSALM 30:12

Even in eternity, you will be thanking God. The appreciation of God's mercy by His people never stops. Without His grace, we would be forever separated from Him, lost in the cares of sin and a hellish existence. The bliss of a heavenly eternity could not be our inheritance. Could you thank Jesus too much now? Or could you ever find enough words to show Him your love? Maybe it's time to get started on your eternal appreciation of your Lord.

Day 353
APPRECIATION OVERFLOW

Continue to live your lives in [Jesus],
rooted and built up in him, strengthened
in the faith as you were taught,
and overflowing with thankfulness.
COLOSSIANS 2:6–7

Strong Christians are thankful Christians. As we realize all Jesus has sacrificed for us and appreciate our inability to live the Christian life on our own, we remember to praise our Savior for His grace. Today, we can be rooted in Jesus, strong in our faith, and thankful to the One who has given us these blessings. Let's overflow with appreciation!

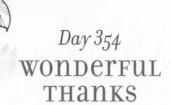

Day 354
WONDERFUL THANKS

Oh, give thanks to the Lord, for He is good!
For His mercy endures forever.
PSALM 136:1 NKJV

Now, honestly, how do you respond to this call for thanks? Does your heart leap at the opportunity, or does it just hit you with a dull thud? Why is it so important to thank God? Because He will always be merciful to you. Whether you rejoice easily or hit the floor with a thud, if you have trusted in the Savior, He still loves you. Isn't that something wonderful to give thanks for?

Day 355
GOD CALLS US TO JOY

Consider it pure joy, my brothers and sisters,
whenever you face trials of many kinds.

JAMES 1:2

Joy? To be faced with trials should cause us joy? Hard to imagine, isn't it? But God calls us to joy when unbelievers persecute us because of our faith or when our situation is merely difficult. It is a joy to Him that we have stood firm in faith, and He calls us to share His delight. That doesn't mean we seek out trials but that we face the situation hand in hand with God. In trials, our spiritual strength increases.

Day 356
LOOK AHEAD
TO HEAVEN

For our light and momentary troubles
are achieving for us an eternal glory
that far outweighs them all.
2 CORINTHIANS 4:17

What trouble could you face on earth that will
not seem small in heaven? No pain from this
life will impede you there. Blessing for faithful service to God will replace each heartache
that discourages you today. When trials and
troubles beset you, look ahead to heaven. Jesus
promises you an eternal reward if you keep
your eyes on Him.

Day 357
JOY IS STRAIGHT AHEAD

The genuineness of your faith, being much more precious than gold that perishes, though it is tested by fire, may be found to praise, honor, and glory at the revelation of Jesus Christ.

1 PETER 1:7 NKJV

Trials have a purpose in our lives. As a smith heats up gold to purify it, God heats up our lives to make spiritual impurities rise to the surface. If we cooperate with Him, sin is skimmed off our lives, purifying our faith. Cleansed lives bring glory to God and joy to us. If a trial lies before you today, envision the joy ahead.

Day 358

HOPE IN GOD ALONE

Because of the LORD's great love we are not consumed, for his compassions never fail.

LAMENTATIONS 3:22

Despite his deep troubles, as Jeremiah sorrowed over Judah's exile, hope remained in his heart. Though he and his nation faced terrible trials, the prophet understood that God would still uphold them. God's compassion never fails His hurting people.

No matter how we struggle, we share the prophet's hope. God alone comforts our hearts as we stumble along a rocky trail.

Day 359
HIS CONCERN

The righteous cry out, and the LORD hears,
and delivers them out of all their troubles.
PSALM 34:17 NKJV

As God's child, you have His ear 24-7 if only
you will pray. Every need, trouble, or praise is
His concern. And not only will He hear about
your trials; He will deliver you from them.
Feel discouraged in your troubles? You need
not stay that way. Just spend time with Jesus.
His help is on the way.

Day 360
WISDOM IN GOD

*Wisdom is the principal thing;
therefore get wisdom: and with
all thy getting get understanding.*
PROVERBS 4:7 KJV

Have you ever thought of yourself as wise? The
Bible says you can be. You don't need a lot of
education or a certain IQ. Real wisdom is found
in God. Simply obey your Lord's commandments, and make knowing Him well your first
priority. Seek after wisdom, and you will find
it in Him. As you daily search for truth in the
Word, your understanding grows.

Day 361
greater ways

For since, in the wisdom of God, the world through wisdom did not know God, it pleased God through the foolishness of the message preached to save those who believe.

1 CORINTHIANS 1:21 NKJV

To this world, God's wisdom doesn't look very wise. Anyone who denies Jesus is blind to the depth of insight God showed in sending His Son to die for us and then raising Him from the dead. But those who accept His sacrifice understand that God's ways are greater than ours, and His astuteness far outweighs our own. As His wisdom fills our once-foolish lives, we gain a new perspective on His perception.

Day 362

WISE HUMILITY

*Woe unto them that are wise in their
own eyes, and prudent in their own sight!*
ISAIAH 5:21 KJV

Wisdom without humility isn't wisdom at all.
When we feel astute under our own power, we
are actually in big trouble and are heading
into foolishness! The truly wise person recognizes that all wisdom comes from God, not frail
humans. As we tap into His mind and connect
with His astuteness, we are wise indeed. There
is no one wiser than He.

Day 363
WISE WORDS

*She speaks with wisdom, and faithful
instruction is on her tongue.*
PROVERBS 31:26

The virtuous woman's mouth speaks kindly wisdom. Hers is no sharp tongue that destroys relationships. As we seek to do God's will, truthful yet caring speech must be ours. Wise words heal hurting hearts. If we have trouble knowing what words bring God's healing, we need only ask Him to let His Spirit bring wisdom and kindness to our mouths and tongues. When we speak as His Spirit directs, we are wise indeed.

Day 364
seek counsel

The way of a fool is right in his own eyes,
but he who heeds counsel is wise.
Proverbs 12:15 NKJV

Listening to others who are wise brings us
wisdom too. Before we make serious choices,
we need to seek the counsel of others. How
can we recognize the wise ones? Those who
have experience and faith and who have made
decisions that blessed their lives can pass their
wisdom to us. Is there some wise person you
need to consult now?

Day 365
SHINE ON

"You are the light of the world.
A town built on a hill cannot be hidden."
MATTHEW 5:14

God means you to be a light set where the world can see it clearly—not a hidden flame behind closed doors, with curtains drawn. Being a light isn't always easy—people see everything you do, and they don't always like it. Don't let the critics stop you. Your works were ordained to glorify God, not to make people comfortable. Knowing that, are you ready to shine today?

scripture index

Psalms

Proverbs